THE
NEW JERSEY
BOAT FISHERMAN

THE
NEW JERSEY
BOAT FISHERMAN

THE COMPLETE INSHORE AND
OFFSHORE GUIDEBOOK TO 50 SALTWATER
HOT SPOTS W/GPS, LORAN, LAYOUT, AND TIPS

NICK HONACHEFSKY

BURFORD BOOKS

Printed in the United States of America.

10 9 8 7 6 5 4 3 2 1

Library of Congress Cataloging-in-Publication Data
      Honachefsky, Nick.
      NJ boat fisherman / Nick Honachefsky.
         p.   cm.
      ISBN 1-58080-133-1
      1. Saltwater fishing—New Jersey. I. Title.

SH525.H66   2005
639.2'2'0916346—dc22

                              2005014615

DEDICATION

A fishing rod and shotgun were placed in my hands by my father and mother at the earliest possible age. Fishing and hunting were an integral part of my education, where the true process of learning respect begins. Sloshing through mud puddles, Red Devil spoon hooked on a 5 foot, ultralight Kunnan rod, and running down to the edge of Spruce Run Reservoir with my two Labradors Skeet and Rink galloping by my side, I would wet a line before school. That's where it began. But if it wasn't for my Babchi, (that's Polish for grandmother) hunting my cousin Tom, brother Bill, and me down twenty years ago when we went AWOL from Thanksgiving dinner, walking three miles and fish a secret spot, then I may not be writing this book today. Because when she left the empty dinner table and tracked us down, steaming mad in her Volkswagen bug, all she saw was three kids skipping along the roadside back to home with smiles on their faces, each holding a 20-pound carp. She could've put an end to that madness right there. She didn't.

With that said, it all comes down to this dedication to my family—all my love, respect and thanks go to my father, Bill, for taking me to fish Island Beach State Park for stripers when I was six, to my brother, Bill Jr., for keeping me in check over the years, and to my mother, Bonnie, for writing the sick notes needed in grade school to play hooky all fishing season long. Now look what you've created.

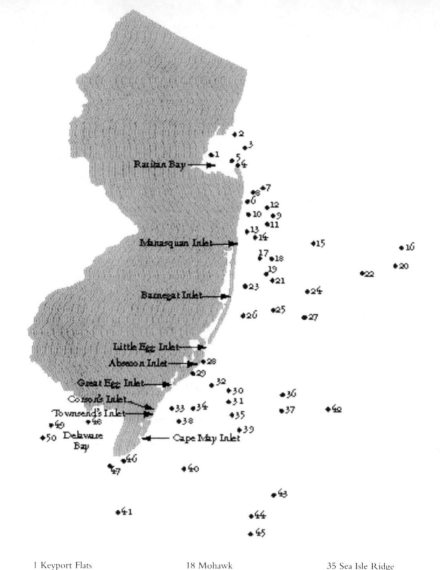

1 Keyport Flats	18 Mohawk	35 Sea Isle Ridge
2 Old Orchard	19 Seaside Lump	36 28-Mile Wreck
3 Romer Shoal	20 Texas Tower #4	37 Cigar
4 Sandy Hook Rip	21 Tolten Lump	38 5 Fathom Bank
5 Flynns Knoll	22 Chicken Canyon	39 East Lump
6 Shrewsbury Rocks	23 Barnegat Light Reef	40 Cape May Reef
7 17 Fathom Bank	24 Resor Wreck	41 Old Grounds
8 Sandy Hook Artificial Reef	25 Barnegat Ridge	42 Lobster Claw
9 Monster Ledge	26 Harvey Cedars Lump	43 Elephant's Trunk
10 England Banks	27 The Fingers	44 19-Fathom Lump
11 Shark River Reef	28 Brigantine Shoal	45 Hot Dog
12 Arundo	29 Lucy the Elephant	46 Eph Shoal
13 Klondike	30 Great Egg Reef	47 Prissywick Shoal
14 Sea Girt Reef	31 Dog Lump	48 60-Foot Slough
15 Glory Hole	32 Tabletop	49 Horseshoe
16 Bacardi	33 Sea Isle Lump	50 Pin Top
17 Manasquan Ridge	34 Avalon Shoal	

Contents

ACKNOWLEDGMENTS

In writing this guide to the best fishing locations I knew I was getting into some tricky territory. To say that the fishing community is tight-lipped about fishing hot-spots is an understatement. But for this undertaking, I was very fortunate to find tackle-shop owners, charter and party boat captains, and individual fishermen who were willing to share their extensive knowledge with me—and for that, I thank them sincerely. They include: Bernie Walker, Lou Grazioso, Pete Kwolek, Bob Balewicz, Bob Konz, John Sowerby, Chris Salus, Bryan Dileo, Sam Rescigno, Steve Nagiewicz and www.njscuba.com, Phil Sciortino Jr., Wayne Bushnell, Darren Dorris, Willie Egerter, Butch Egerter, Bobby Bogan, Howard Bogan, Sean Reilly, Pete Barrett, Bill Figley of the Division of Fish and Game's Reef Building fund, Rich and Bob Przewoznik, George Algard, Ed Bronstein, Mike Haluska, Gene Nigro, Jim Hutchinson, Jr., Dave Showell, Eric Kuenhart, Jim Wallace, Don Brown, Matt Slobodjian, Chris "River Rat" Lido, Dave DeGennaro, Austin Perilli, and Matt Durando. I also want to thank saltwater journalist icons Al Ristori and John Geiser, who keep our sport alive and kicking, publisher Peter Burford for entertaining this idea of mine, and each of the editors I write for who have faith in my work. And lastly, I want to thank you, the reader, for continuing to promote the finest sport on the planet.

All right, you can drop the lines in now!

INTRODUCTION

I've always hustled to find the hot saltwater fishing spots. You'd discuss the topic with friends late at night, ask around at the local bait shops in the morning, hound captains mid-afternoon at the dock, all to get an edge, so the next day you could put a respectable catch together. As a kid, there wasn't much of a game plan when I went fishing. My friend Lido and I would take the 14-foot aluminum Grumman, and launch into Raritan Bay with a rusted-out 1960 6.0 HP Johnson on the back. We'd putter around the bay, white smoke spewing out of the Johnson, with nothing but a few busted fluke rigs, a bucket of killies draped over the side and some prayers. We had no real idea where to go—off the Ammo pier, across from the Coast Guard station—how 'bout here? Just drop 'em in, man. Being fairly competent anglers even at 17, we'd manage to pull a few dozen flatties out of the big bay, bag the keepers, and motor in at about a half-knot's pace, battling against the outgoing tide for a two-hour ride back to the trailer. Life was hard back then, but good.

It's better today. We've got bigger boats, faster engines, and believe it or not, now we know where we're going, what we're going for, and what we need to prepare when we wake up in the morning. Why? Because of some unselfish individuals who, throughout the years, have readily shared all kinds of fishing information with us. It's been a circular learning process that feeds off itself, gaining and giving information. But what does it translate into? Quite simply, for those in the circle, more fish caught, better use of time, and more stories to talk about with the bumps at the local watering hole, with your cousin at a family function, or with the guy pumping your gas at the Mobil.

This book is a guide to all in the circle who have the desire, drive and dedication to put every available moment out in the salt. It has been written to help you to create memories that will last a lifetime, to bring a communal feeling of brotherhood amongst anglers of all reaches, and of course, to put more fish in the cooler. Dog-ear it, leave it under the console, mark it up, do whatever you want to do with it; just catch some fish and have a fine time doing it. And if you see two determined kids hitting the salt in a ramshackle boat with a smoking motor making a run for it, give 'em some room and get outta their way!

LEGEND

GBT	— Giant Bluefin Tuna		COD	— Cod
STB	— Striped Bass		BLK	— Blackfish
SHK	— Shark (Mako, Tiger, Blue, Thresher, Brown, Dusky)		LNG	— Ling
			LTY	— Little Tunny
BLF	— Bluefish		TRG	— Triggerfish
WEK	— Weakfish		DPH	— Dolphin
POR	— Porgy		SKP	— Skipjack
POL	— Pollock		SPN	— Spanish Mackerel
SEB	— Sea Bass		WHM	— White Marlin
FLK	— Fluke		BKD	— Black Drum
BFT	— Bluefin Tuna		MCK	— Mackerel
YFT	— Yellowfin Tuna		CRK	— Croaker
BET	— Bigeye Tuna		CON	— Conger Eel
WFL	— Winter Flounder		OPT	— Ocean Pout

1

Keyport Flats

GPS: 40'26.71 / 74'12.15
LORAN: 27082 / 43714
Distance: One-third mile out off Buoy 3 from base of Keyport Public Launch Ramp
Depth: 12 to 20 feet
Target Species: Winter Flounder, Striped Bass
Prime Time of Year: Late March through mid-May (WFL), mid-April through mid-June (STB)

In recent years, a real treasure chest has opened up for Jersey winter flounder fishermen. Way back inside Raritan Bay a one-half to one mile stretch of muddy shoal bottom, known as the Keyport Flats, hosts an enviable population of winter flounder during the early spring months. Bearing 20 degrees from Keyport harbor, Keyport Flats sits off the bayshore beaches of Cliffwood Beach and stretches from Union Beach to Morgan Inlet.

Chris Salus of Crabby's Bait and Tackle considers the Flats a mainstay for his spring fishery. "The Flats comprise about a

200-acre section, and the bottom is a soft, black mud which the blackback flounder sink themselves into. When the water temps hit 46 degrees, the flounder start to get on the bite. The area here averages from 16 to 18 feet of water, with occasional spots of 12 to 14 feet. This is where the water warms up first coming out of the winter months. The flounder rest on the flats and where the shallow black mud warms up the water."

One key attraction on the Keyport Flats is the presence of an artificial oyster reef that rests on the north side of the flats and is marked by a yellow buoy. The NJ/NY Baykeeper's Association has been sinking discarded oyster shells from local restaurants to rebuild the oyster reefs that were once prominent in the bay area. Baby oysters are then placed by the Baykeepers there to root themselves and grow. An adult oyster filters over 50 gallons of water per day, and provides an endless food supply for foraging species.

Mid-March through early May will hold the flounder in the flats, and the outgoing tide produces better, as the warmer water flows out from the back. The mud holds an array of tapeworms, sandworms, bloodworms, mantis and grass shrimp, mussels and clams, and the flowing tide propels this buffet past the waiting flounder. The best bet is to find a small sloping shelf, such as a depth change from 12 to 15 feet, and set up anchor there on the upslope or downslope where flounder will be waiting.

Coinciding with the exodus of the flounder run, striped bass overlap and move in during late April and early May. The bass will hunt and feed on the flounder on the flats, but most of the time, as the water temps hover in the mid-50s, a well-established clam slick and fresh clam baits will bring bass to the boat. Stripers at this time of year usually range from 22 to 30 inches, as the smaller bass are the first to move into the backwaters to feed. Many times, when clamming with chum pots and fresh clams, a rod stuck out the side and bouncing the bottom will take a fair share of flounder while you are reeling in bass after bass. Maximize your time and fish for both species in the springtime months.

Access to the Keyport Flats can be reached easily with a trailered boat from the Keyport municipal harbor or Keyport public ramp at end of American Legion Drive.

HOT SHOT TIP

When anchored, sink down a chum pot filled with clam or mussel bricks at the bow of the boat so the chum settles at the stern. Bring a sash weight to drop down and stir up mud below, releasing worms, crabs and bugs for added flounder chum.

2

Old Orchard Lighthouse

GPS: 40'30.73 / 74.05.92
LORAN: 27047 / 43749
Distance: 3 miles out from Keyport #3 Can, 2.3 miles from Great Kills Harbor
Depth: 19 to 32 feet
Target Species: Striped Bass
Prime Time of Year: Late April through June

Know this—when the big striped bass move in to play ball, you can bet that they will be hanging around the area of Old Orchard Lighthouse. Why? Come late April, immense schools of adult menhaden make their push into Raritan Bay and try to move far back into the backwater estuary to spawn. A very attractive spot for the bunker to do their deed is the Great Kills Harbor, off of Staten Island, NY. When these bunker stack up, you'll think you could walk on water across their backs.

When they finish up, they begin to filter out from the back, and then it's a free-for-all. Bluefish begin the carnage, slicing two pound bunker clean in half, with bass underneath sucking down the scraps and picking off live ones as the schools of menhaden frantically run around for their lives. I've fished this area year after year, and it's a sad stage for the bunker. It can get downright crazy, with the blitzing conditions of huge bluefish and bass, and then with overeager boat fishermen. You've got to try and mind your manners here. Once you see someone find a bunker school, don't motor up right next to him and chase the bunker away. Stay on the outskirts maybe 75 yards away and try to snag or cast net a few, otherwise the bunker will be chased out of the area. Trust me, heed this advice, or you'll probably get some Jersey-fueled bank sinkers heading toward your boat.

Once you've got a healthy supply of live bunker in your livewell, fish on the Jersey side of the lighthouse by staying on

Live bunker are silver candy for Raritan Bay striped bass. Cast net a few dozen, put them in a livewell, hook them behind the dorsal fin, and send 'em down to the stripers.

the south side, since the lighthouse marks the demarcation line of New Jersey and New York. The water on the Jersey side will range from 19 to 30 feet. Search around until you find some marks on the bottom that show bass collecting on various underwater sandy humps, and get ready to rumble. Drop a whole, live bunker down to the bottom on a fishfinder slide rig with an ample 5 to 6 foot, 30 to 40-pound fluorocarbon leader and a size 6/0 Gamakatsu circle or Octopus hook. Stripers and blues will be on it within seconds if they are in the area. During mid-May, you'll have to wade through surges of big blues in the 5- to 18-pound class if you want to fish for a 20- to 40-pound bass. This fishery peaks in the month of May but will start at the end of April and run sometimes through the end of June. I'm pumped up just writing about this one! You've got to see it for yourself.

A point worthy of noting here is that the stripers you will be tying into are either on their way to spawn or have spent their eggs and are on their way back. The bass pursuing the live bunker will generally be in the 25- to 50-pound class, which are the female breeders. I strongly recommend the release of these fish, and the use of circle hooks if you plan on releasing them, unless you are quick on the hookset with a J-Hook. Take a snapshot and release her back into the water.

HOT SHOT TIP

When you feel that live bunker get antsy and vibrating underwater, he's being watched in a bad way. Wait to feel a thump-thump, and let the bass take the bait and run off if you are using circle hooks, and simply reel up tight to set the hook; if you are using J-Hooks, set the hook on the first bump.

3

Romer Shoal

GPS: 40 31.00 / 73 60.00
LORAN: 26995 / 43740
Distance: 2.3 miles from #17 buoy off Sandy Hook
Depth: 3.5 to 26 feet
Target Species: Striped Bass, Bluefish, Blackfish
Prime Time of Year: Late April through June (STB, BLF, BLK)

Romer Shoal is one of those spots that is both easily recognizable and productive. With a lighthouse that stands 54 feet tall marking the general area, it shouldn't be too hard to find. Sitting about 200 yards southeast of the Romer Shoal lighthouse, channel markers indicate the north side of shoal, which encompasses a circular area roughly a few hundred yards square. The 6S buoy lies on the east side, Romer Lighthouse is on the northwest side, Swash Channel on the southwest, and Ambrose Channel on the northeast side. Running over the waters with a depthfinder, you will notice where the waters rise from 26-foot depths to the 10- to 12-foot range. Most water surrounding the shoal runs from 26 to 28 feet, and the edges of the roundish shoal hover around the

12-foot average. But the sands are ever-shifting here, and on low tides, you can find even thinner water depths of 5 to 8 feet, which can pose a minor worry, as breaking waves will form on outgoing tides when the heaving water hits the shoal.

Probably the most influential factor in fishing the shoal area is the presence of strong currents, as it's basically in the dead center of the outflow and inflow of the Atlantic Ocean and Raritan Bay. Springtime is a good bet for a first shot to set up for striped bass, when water temps hits the high 50s and low 60s. Though most bass taken from this area run from schoolie size of 18 to 20 inches up to 30 inches, you don't usually see any truly large cows sticking around. Captain Gene Nigro of the *Phantom* has a favorite spot to set up for bass: "On the Jersey side of the Romer lighthouse, there's a little rocky cove that boats belonging to workers at the lighthouse tie up on. When the outgoing tide flows against this protective jetty, a great rip starts swirling on the east side of the jetty outcropping. We troll

Al Ristori and Lou Grazioso of Stripermania *get in on the early season striper action on Romer Shoal. The springtime bass are suckers for a fresh clam bait.*

six- inch wooden plugs on the outside of the swirls and score tons of bass when this condition unfolds."

Trolling plugs produces, but the main game to tackle the early season stripers here revolves around dropping fresh clam baits, and you have to consider the current. Captain Pete Kwolek of the *Hook 'em Up* hits the shoal with one constant in mind—"Bring a ton of chum. The current really rips and you'll go through bags quite fast. The key is to get set up on anchor before the tide rips to establish a clam slick underneath the boat and keep the bass close, but when the tide pulls in or out, your slick will dissipate quicker and further back. Try and hit the area an hour or two either end of high tide, because the current won't be as swift, and your baits will be below you instead of miles behind."

And the current can really rush here. On one trip with Kwolek in mid May, we had to let out over 100 yards of line, just to get the clams back to where the slick was settling. We had 10 ounces of weight on, and still couldn't hold until we had that enormous distance and scope of line out. Besides bass, you cannot overlook the blackfishing opportunity in the spring months as 7- to 8-pound tautog can be muscled out of the lighthouse rocks on clams and green crabs. Bluefish will come ripping through in force during the May tide changes, slicing your lines with a vengeance, so it's best to have a few rigs pre-tied. And one more thing—if you notice some explosions around your boat during the spring months, likened to depth charges going off, try and pay attention, because if you catch it right, you'll see 5 to 10 foot Atlantic Sturgeon vaulting out of the water! It's no joke!

HOT SHOT TIP

Tie on an extra long, 10 foot piece of 30 pound of fluorocarbon leader to your main line, so that when bluefish bite you off, you can cut the shredded line and snell a hook immediately on the end.

4

Sandy Hook Rip

GPS: 40'28.50 / 74.00.10
LORAN: 27005 / 43723
Distance: From Tip of Sandy Hook out 400 yards
Depth: 7 to 32 feet
Target Species: Striped Bass, Bluefish, Fluke, Weakfish
Prime Time of Year: May through November (STB) (BLF),
   May through October (FLK) May, June (WEK)

Take a prolific bay and a fertile ocean, stick a flowing channel in between them, and what do you get? You get a waterway where the bounty of the ocean flows in and out on every ebb and waning tide, funneling in baitfish, crabs, sea bugs and all sorts of aquatic morsels for gamefish to feed on. It's like striking a vein of gold. Sound too good to be true? It isn't. In fact, its proper name is the Sandy Hook Rip.

   Just as the name suggests, incoming and outgoing tides shift the underwater sands of this piece of real estate, making the average depths change from time to time. But for practical purposes, the actual rip where the most wave action occurs rests less than a hundred yards north off of Sandy Hook, and during tide changes ranges between 14 and 17 feet as it runs west to east, dropping into a depth of between 26 and 28 feet to as deep as 32 feet by the 11 buoy. Sandy Hook Channel lies on the north side of the Rip and the skinniest depths rise from 7 to 11 feet between buoy 11 and the Sandy Hook Channel on the southwest side, right off the tip of the Hook.

HOT SHOT TIP

Fish the Rip during the night in the summertime with live eels. The deeper waters will hold larger 20 to 30-pound stripers.

The Rip is a magnet for striped bass, bluefish and fluke throughout the spring, summer and fall months, following the smorgasbord of baitfish, crabs, and sea bugs that flow in and out with the ripping tides. All migratory species pass through the rip, taking advantage of the wild influx and outflow of fare, and will usually stick around through many tides, feeding upon the abundance of food.

Mainly, October and November are the prime times to fish the Rip for the targeted striped bass. The beauty of the Rip is that even though it is best fished from a vessel, it can be reached by a strong surfcaster. Captain Pete Kwolek of the *Hook 'em Up* has a sure-fire striper rig which tallies up hundreds of bass each season. Kwolek employs a 3-way swivel: one eye for the running line, one eye with a 36-inch, 30-pound piece of fluorocarbon snelled with a 4/0 #92641 Baitholder hook, and on the final eye, a 12 to 16-inch dropper loop for a 3 to 8-ounce bank sinker. The finest bait to put on your hook at this time is the sandworm, as they flutter nicely but keep on the hook in the rippy waters.

Since most species indulge themselves and filter in and out with the strong currents and pull of the Rip's waters, during the migratory months some unusual species will get caught up in the pull. Here's a quick story. One morning while fishing with my father in late May, his reel went singing, and after regaining the line to boatside, we saw a big, brown torpedo on the end. That was the last we saw of a 50-pound cobia before it took off and sent the line snapping!

5

Flynn's Knoll

GPS: 40'29.00 / 74'01.50
LORAN: 27010 / 43726
Distance: Half-mile North off tip of Sandy Hook
Depth: 15 to 30 feet
Target Species: Striped Bass, Summer Flounder, Weakfish
Prime Time of Year: April through June (STB), May through September
(FLK)(POR), July/August (WEK)

In northern Jersey, anglers know of the red-hot productive grounds called Flynn's Knoll. Flynn's Knoll is bordered by the Sandy Hook Channel on its south side, the Chapel Hill Channel on the west side and the Swash on the north side. Captain Phil Sciortino of the *Tackle Box* attributes it's fantastic action to its location among these channels—a shallow area surrounded by deep water on all sides. The Knoll is loaded with crusty mussel beds, and flushes bait in and out with every tide.

Captain Phil and his family have plied these waters for generations and have reaped the rewards of year-round fun. In the spring months of April and May, stripers and weakfish with big shoulders run through the area. The best spot is by the 14 and 16 buoys where the bottom rises to 20 feet and even up to 15 to 17 feet. Captain Phil notes, "A 3-way swivel with a 1-foot dropper for a bank sinker, and a 3 or 4-foot fluorocarbon leader with a 3/0 baitholder on the business end does the trick here. Because of the current, the sandworm flutters nicely. Thread one sandworm onto the hook and then lance on one or two more through the head."

HOT SHOT TIP

Don't be shy, hook two to three sandworms on at a time, the first one threaded, and the next two hooked by their heads. A triple teaser of sands flutters like candy for a bass or tiderunner weakfish.

During the late spring and through the summer, the stripers tend to react better to clam baits and bunker chunks on the same type of three-way rig. When this occurs, hit up the middle of the knoll near the fish pots just north of the 16 buoy. Drop your clams and bunker here, and if you want to target bluefish as well, start up a little clam or bunker chunk slick to bring them in and hold them. July and August continue to bring in the weakfish, and they love to rip into sandworms. However, in the past year the heat of the summer has also brought in an immense population of porgies, who will make it tough for you to get to the bottom, but will give you non-stop action. To target the porgies, scale down your hooks to a 1/0 baitholder and use only bits of worms.

When the waters cool in the fall, the bass are still on the bite, but the bait of choice turns to eels. Use a four-foot fluoro-carbon leader with a barrel swivel and 4/0 or 5/0 live bait hook on the end and employ an egg sinker on the sliding part of the line. Hook the eel through the bottom lip and out the eye. For the night time eel fishery, hot pieces of turf exist in deeper water around the 10 buoy and double sticks of the Range Towers where the water hits a 30 foot depth, and also by the 8S buoy and Single Sticks area, where there's a 20 to 30 foot drop.

6

Shrewsbury Rocks

GPS: 40'20.29 / 73'57.50
LORAN: 26950 / 43635
Distance: 9.5 miles north from Shark River Inlet
Depth: 14 to 43 feet
Target Species: Striped Bass, Blackfish
Prime Time of Year: May/June–October through December (STB)
   October through December (BLK)

There flat-out isn't another spot so striped bass-friendly as the Shrewsbury Rocks. The Rocks, as they are affectionately known, are a rocky and rolling submarine reef running east to northeast that anchors bass to the area. During the striped bass spring and fall migration, the stony underwater structure draws bass like a magnet where they set up shop to feed on, hide from and ambush prey. The prominently defined subterranean mountains average in depth of 20 to 30 feet, but on the north side there is a rock hill that rises abruptly from 42 to 15 feet—a wall of solid rock. This spot is termed the "Elbow," and is notorious as a bass hangout. On the western side of the Rocks lies an area called the "Ribbons" that rises up to 14 feet and undulates on the fishfinder screen. Running only a few hundred yards from the Ribbons to the west, you will launch off the ledge and drop immediately to 28 feet. The way eastern outer edge of the Rocks is marked by the green bell buoy and depth hits 43 feet there. An inside green can marks the 26 foot depth on the eastern edge of the main portion of the rocks. The two cans are monuments that most boaters focus on to begin their day out, by trolling between the two on an east to west course, figure-eighting back and forth.

HOT SHOT TIP

For bunker spooning, grab two nine-foot bunker spoon rods, and set up with a 4/0 size reel spooled with 200 feet of wire connected via barrel swivel to a 12 to 20-foot 80-pound leader, with a ball bearing swivel on the end.

The Rocks are best known for the world-class bass fishing during the seasonal migration. Striped bass in the spring fly by the area to fill up on bunker schools and lay their eggs, and in the fall, they head again southward to warmer waters. The presence of breeder, cow bass makes the Rocks a trophy fishery. While bass average 12 to 20 pounds here, 25 to 40-pounders are not uncommon and the 40 to 50-plus size bass are taken with unusual consistency. In fact, in 2004, if you didn't catch a 30 to 40-pound bass at the Rocks, you just weren't putting in enough time!

At the Rocks, it's all about trolling. During the fall migration of stripers, the fleet trolling the area resembles a bunch of drunken ships aimlessly cruising around at slow speeds, zigzagging in circles with lines out the back. But, in all the apparent chaos, it seems to work with very few tangles or altercations. Two of the hottest methods to tackle the behemoth bass are by trolling bunker spoons and by dragging shad spreader bar rigs. Captain Lou Grazioso of *Stripermania* employs both methods when working over the area. "Shad bar rigs are like soft candy for sweet-toothed stripers. The rig is designed to give the presentation of a school of bunker swimming enticingly through the water column. The shad bar usually contains six 6-inch shads and sometimes trail with a stinger type shad about 10 to 12 inches long set at the back. The shads actually swim like a school and the trailer shad lagging behind usually ignites the 'survival of the fittest' mechanism in a striper and will most times be the one that gets pummeled by a bass. I like using Chartreuse and Alewife, or Chartreuse/Solid Green colorings. You want to let out the shad bar rig approximately 50 to 100 yards back off of the stern and troll between three and four knots."

Shad spreader bars usually attract the 15 to 25-pound fish, but historically, when anglers want to take a shot at the title on the Rocks, they break out the bunker spoons. Certain spoons to use include a size #1 Julian's Montauk Bunker Spoon in White and Green Chartreuse or any number of other spoons from reputable manufacturers such as the Old Reliable and Crippled Alewife. Trolling the bunker spoons is an art form and must be done correctly for them to work properly. Grazioso states, "Start your troll somewhere between 2.8 and 3.5 knots and let out about 150 feet of the wire. The key to this technique is to watch the tips of the rods as you troll. Look for a steady heartbeat throbbing type of rhythm that goes bump-bump-bump-bump consistently. That spoon will transmit this heartbeat to the tip of the rod when it is wafting through the water in a balanced and true fashion. If at any time you see an irregular rhythm, such as the rod double pumping or twitching irregularly, the spoon may be rolling over or may be tangled. Give the line a hard pull with your hands or reel it in and let it out again if you need to set the spoon true."

Trolling the Shrewsbury Rocks is a learned exercise, as some pieces of rock jut up faster than you can maneuver around. Inevitably, you will get hung up and most likely lose a few expensive spreader bars and bunker spoons. Make a note on the MOB button where you hit the snags, and try to get by the sides of them instead of over them to find the big bass.

7

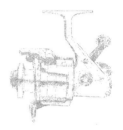

17 Fathom Bank

GPS: 40'23.05 / 73'48.54
LORAN: 26889 / 43655
Distance: 9.5 miles southeast from Sandy Hook
Depth: 94 to 114 feet
Target Species: Bluefish, Blackfish
Prime Time of Year: Late May through October (BLF),
   October through January (BLK, LNG)

"Ahoy! Drop 'er to seventeen fathoms!" Invariably, that was what the old, salty dory fishermen said to each other as they hit this prolific area to fish the famed 17 Fathom Bank. Truly, it has a captivating quality. 17 Fathoms is nestled on the upper west end of the Mud Hole, where the beginning of the Mud starts grooving its underwater trench, which is the prehistoric, subterranean extension of the Hudson River channel. Right on the spot, water depth runs from 94 feet down to a fairly obvious 102 feet (actually 17 fathoms) but the immediate surrounding area can vary in depth 104 to 114 feet, and even drop down to 128 feet just within a half mile or less to the east. What makes 17 fathoms so fish-friendly is the combination of shifting water depths combined with the eclectic bounty of bottom structure that blankets the area. It's a virtual rocky road of natural broken bottom, with stretches of mussel beds, barnacles, snails, and clam beds. Then, on top of all the natural stuff, there is a massive amount of man-made material around the area, most notably the rubble from the construction of the Holland Tunnel and subway systems of New York City.

Bluefish are the ticket here. If you've ever spent any time bluefishing on any party boat from the Highlands down through Barnegat, you can be almost certain that at one point, you fished the 17 Fathom bank. Usually, a week before Memorial Day kicks off the push when bluefish bring on the heat. June is the prime time to bag bluefish from tailor size of two to three pounds to alligator size of 15 to 20 pounds. The cool thing is, the bluefish blitz can happen at any hour of the day or night, and many party boat captains run around the clock to put their fares into action. When the sun is up, metal jigs such as Ava A27 to A67 jigs, as well as Crippled Herring jigs to four ounces produce loads of blue dogs. Be sure to either bulk up with 40 pound plus leader or a steel wire leader to attach your jig; otherwise, consider it gone. Night-time trips revolve around the chunk bite with a nice, smelly bunker slick and an eight inch steel-leadered 5/0 Mustad #92641 Baitholder hook with a three to four inch bunker back lanced on. The trick here is to keep your baits flowing with the speed of the slick. You may need to pinch on a rubbercore sinker above the leader, or even thread on an egg sinker from one-quarter to two ounces to get the chunk to fall with the speed of the slick. Daytime bluefish trips are underscored by catches of little tunny or false albacore during the months of August and September, and smaller metals such as Ava 007's cast to them and retrieved at a lightning pace will turn their heads for a strike.

The abundant structure below houses a formidable array of blackfish during the colder months of November through early January, as well as ling, when the water temperatures hover in the 42 to 50-degree range. The concrete rubble, and other assorted mix of structure at 17 Fathoms will rise six or seven feet up off bottom, and fortunately it's not a "sticky" type of structure, so you won't lose many rigs dropping down for tautog and ling.

HOT SHOT TIP

When jigging, you need to find where the blues are hanging in the water column. Immediately drop your metal jig to the bottom, then reel in 10 feet at a time, stop and try jigging for a minute, then repeat the process until you get whacked.

8

Sandy Hook Artificial Reef

GPS: 40'22.20 / 73'56.20 approximate center
LORAN: 26943 / 43647
Distance: 11.3 miles from Shark River, 17.9 miles from Manasquan, 5.2 miles from Sandy Hook
Depth: 40 to 60 feet
Target Species: Blackfish, Fluke, Sea Bass, Porgy
Prime Time of Year: Late March through May, November (BLK), May through October (POR, FLK, SEB)

New Jersey's Division of Fish and Wildlife's Reef Program is heralded as one of the best in the world, and, led by Bill Figley, New Jersey anglers now have 14 full-blooded reef sites that span our coastline. The man-made structure, combined with natural underwater terrain and shipwrecks, all combine to support diverse marine life from phytoplankton to Giant Bluefin tuna. Reef sites provide an incredible opportunity for the boat fisherman, and the Sandy Hook Reef Site is a great place to start, since it is New Jersey's oldest reef site, taking its first deposits in 1937.

Hard-pulling, bulldog blackfish, a.k.a tautog, are abundant on New Jersey's artificial reef sites, and will readily inhale green crabs or clam baits.

The entire region spans 1.4 square miles and exists the same 1.4 miles off the Sea Bright coastline. The composition of the reef is a combination of long, tumbled masses of broken concrete and bridge rubble and includes sunken ships such as the 110-foot tanker *VL Keegan*, 65-foot tug *Dorothy*, and 45-foot barge *Coleman*. Bill Figley, Reef Program Coordinator, notes: "The Sandy Hook Reef is one of the easiest and closest reef sites to fish. There's over 1,000 rockpiles that are 300 feet long, by 60 feet wide, by 6 feet high on the site. Some of the loads of concrete overlapped when we jettisoned them, so some spots will be higher than 6 feet off the sea floor—look for these higher spots and you'll find better fishing."

The debris field of concrete throughout the site is accentuated by rocky mountains at the east and southeast corners. Most of the concrete debris is found on the northern portion of the site, and the three wrecks are near the southern section. The reef holds fluke, porgies and sea bass in the snags and crags. Figley offers insight into fishing this area. "The north end of the site holds most of the concrete rubble. Find the areas where the piles overlap and create clumps that rise higher than the surrounding concrete. This area in particular is a five-star tog spot around the base structure. Up in the water column along the sides of the piles, giant porgies stick tight."

Another selling point of the Sandy Hook Reef is that it is situated just northwest of the prolific Shrewsbury Rocks, so a day out on the reef can be turned from a bottom fishing trek to a striped bass trolling adventure in an instant.

HOT SHOT TIP

When bottom fishing the concrete rubble for blackfish, tie on a breakaway 10-pound test dropper loop to your original dropper. On a rooted snag, you'll break off the weight, but save the rest of your rig.

9

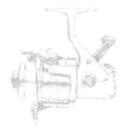

Monster Ledge

GPS: 40 06.80 / 73 33.98
LORAN: 26737 / 43475
Distance: 21.5 miles east/northeast from Manasquan Inlet
Depth: 145 to 250 feet
Target Species: Mako and Thresher Shark, Bonito, Little Tunny, Giant Bluefin Tuna
Prime Time of Year: June through August, (SHK) July through September, (LIT, BON, SKP, BFT) September, October (GBT)

With a name like Monster Ledge, you can't go wrong. Running 21.5 miles out of Manasquan Inlet, you can enter the arena where men are made, dreams are realized or shattered, and legends are born. All right, there may be a bit of hyperbole in there, but where else can you tie into mako sharks over 400 pounds and giant bluefin tuna over 600 pounds? Those reasons right there are enough to justify the name. Monster Ledge is situated at the near uppermost western end of the Mud Hole and its share of the underwater trench spans from 25 to 40 fathoms.

HOT SHOT TIP
If gunning for giants, be prepared to start the engines to chase them down to minimize fighting time and preserve the quality of the meat.

In the 1980's, Monster Ledge was one of the finest sharking and giant tuna spots on the east coast, but commercial long lining decimated a good portion of the shark fishery, and constant commercial pressure by bottom trawlers pretty much erased all the ling and whiting that were once common in the area. The ling and whiting were the main staple of the giant bluefin, and thus when the bait went, so did the giants. But though we went through a drought in the 1990's, there is still hope for tying into a giant bluefin. Captain Dave DeGennaro of the *Hi-Flier* says, "I never go out to the Ledge without being prepared for a giant. We can be out there targeting plenty of small pelagics that call it home, such as bonito, false albacore, and schoolie and medium bluefin of 20 to 100 pounds, but make no mistake, there's always a 130 class setup on board, rigged and ready to go with butterfish chunks for a giant. It's unmistakable when you see the red boomerang on the depth finder, you might think it's a huge school of bait, but it's not. It's much bigger than that." September and October give the angler the best shot in tackling a giant.

But the more abundant monsters that reside with numbers at Monster Ledge are still sharks. Come June, the mako shark fishery opens up, as tinker mackerel, rainfish and other baits mosey their way through the currents of the Mud Hole. DeGennaro points out, "Usually sharks will cut off the bite and continue migrating by mid-July, but Monster Ledge will hold sharks all the way through the summer. In recent times, a lot of threshers have come out of here as well. When other guys are saying there's no sharks around, give it a shot here, and see what you come up with."

The small pelagics (bonito and false albacore) amassing in the area will be convinced to bite with fresh, whole spearing. The Ledge offers a great opportunity to tangle with the speed-sters as well as some quality bluefin on light tackle gear such as a 20-class outfit. Small and medium bluefin will stay all through July and August, and the whole spearing or butterfish chunks will tease them into a bite.

10

England Banks

GPS: 40'14.10 / 73'55.35
LORAN: 26922 / 43570
Distance: 8 miles north from Manasquan Inlet, 3 miles north of Shark River Inlet
Depth: 45 to 60 feet
Target Species: Sea Bass, Fluke, Porgy
Prime Time of Year: June through October (SEB, FLK, POR)

The England Banks are a tried and true year-round fishing ground, easily reached by most boaters. The Banks begin off of Deal and extend northeast up towards Elberon, roughly 2.5 miles off of Elberon Beach, and are a short ride from the Shark River and Manasquan Inlets. The Banks are rocky hills and mussel beds, which border each side of a trough. Capt. Howard Bogan of the 125' *Jamaica* has perused the banks in the past decades to put his fares on plenty of varied fish species. "Back over a decade ago, England Banks used to be an incredible whiting and ling hot spot in the wintertime, but because of the immense overfishing, that has changed over the years. Now, we hit the banks mainly for a good pull of sea bass, during their migration in the spring and fall months." The prime part of the banks run in depth from 52 to 60 feet, and on the east or south edges, it can drop down to the 70-foot range, providing structure not only for sea bass, but fluke as well. Bogan states, "I prefer to fish the banks drifting over them, you get to cover plenty more ground, and the fish are always moving around there. You can anchor up if you want, but you'll only get a quick spurt of action before it's cleaned up. If you drift, you'll constantly keep picking at the fish over the area. You've got to read your fishfinder and constantly look for the bumps on the bottom. Mark them and keep drifting over them."

The England Banks are made up of mussel beds and rocks, and will hold other varieties of species such as blackfish, ling, fluke, and bluefish in some years. "I remember several years back when the sand eels stuck around the banks. We had bluefish penned up there all season and it was a mess of activity on the choppers," Bogan states. Spring sees the sea bass influx, summertime will show the fluke, and the fall months produce blues, some stripers, and sea bass once again. During the winter months, depending on the concentration, you can find ling, and a few remaining blackfish and sea bass. "Whatever species is abundant at the time, the key to fishing the ground successfully is to always be drifting over the ledges and troughs that rise and fall. And be sure to pay attention to the humps and bumps, mark them down and set another drift when you are into some action." Big bucktails here will take big fluke, and be sure to carry an arsenal of medium-size metal jigs, such as the Ava 27 and 47's or 2-ounce Crippled Herrings to catch a cooler full of sea bass. Bounce over ledges and humps, and be sure you are holding ground.

HOT SHOT TIP

Bounce a 2 to 3-ounce chrome ball jig with a squid strip lanced on the hook. The shiny metal will attract sea bass as well as fluke.

11

Shark River Reef

GPS: 40'06.80 / 73'41.40 approximate center
LORAN: 26794 / 43486
Distance: 22.3 miles from Sandy Hook, 15.6 miles from Manasquan, 14.8 miles from Shark River
Depth: 120 to 134 feet
Target Species: Fluke, Bluefish, Blackfish, Sea Bass, Cod, Pollock
Prime Time of Year: May and October (FLK), April through June (BLK, SEB) November through January (COD, POL)

While most of New Jersey's reef sites lie within two to eight miles off the shoreline, only two are considered deepwater type reef sites—the Shark River Reef and Deepwater Reef. The Shark River Reef not only holds the distinction of being the deepest Jersey reef site, with depths reaching 134 feet, but also, according to Bill Figley of NJ's Artificial Reef Program, has the largest volume of natural and artificial material of any reef site in the world. It was built 14.8 miles off the coast, and provides incredibly diverse habitat and cover for a varied assortment of inshore and mid-range species.

The entire area encompasses an area of .72 square miles and harbors sunken tankers, tugboats, and cargo ships. Probably the highlighted shipwreck of the reef is the 460-foot attack cargo transport USS *Algol* near the south side of the reef. Other notable wrecks include the 160-foot oil tanker *Sam Berman*, 250-foot sludge tanker *Coney Island*, and two 174-foot tankers. In 2003, the reef received a welcome addition of subway cars strategically spilled on the north and south ends of the site. The whole northeast quadrant of the reef site is fortified by 26 solid granite rock mountain ridges which jut up from the ocean floor, and each span 500 feet long, 200 feet wide and 40 to 60 feet high. Wow! The eclectic combination of shipwreck, concrete, tire units and rock mountains hail fish from all around to come play in the playground.

HOT SHOT TIP

Shark River Reef was finally finished in early 2005. When marine growth begins to completely blanket the structure below in the next few years, it's going to be the hottest ticket around.

The Shark River Reef is a year-round producer, and species shift in and out with the water temps. Springtime months bring in the inshore migration of sea bass and blackfish back to the structure, as well as large fluke moving back in from their wintering grounds. Early summer the bluefish invasion begins and blues will school up over the reef, and with the bluefish come sharks. Captain Steve Nagiewicz of the dive boat *Diversion II* notes, "When the bluefish are schooling about the reef, sharks start to move in. I've seen mako, blue sharks, tigers and hammerheads down there. Most people don't realize the sharks stay in the area, but when bluefish are there as food, they stick around."

When the fall months roll around, sea bass, bergalls, and bluefish own the site. As the water temps drop in late fall into the low 60s, medium size pollock from five to 15 pounds and ling become hot on the bite. Winter months still hold a large population of ling and a fair show of pollock on the site even into mid-40 degree water, and you will begin to notice the presence of nuclear sized conger eels and wide-mouthed ocean pout, as they hide and stick themselves into the varied structure underneath. Because of strong currents, bottom fishermen usually need to drop down at least an 8-ounce bank sinker and must be prepared to stack on up to 20 ounces of lead to hold.

Sure, a strong current prevails at the site, but nothing has ever been so strong in recorded history as the Nor'easter of 1992. Here's a testament to the awesome power of the ocean. According to Captain Nagiewicz, "The '92 Nor'easter was unprecedented. The swell was so powerful that it pivoted the stern section of the 460 foot USS *Algol* a total distance of over 200 feet. The entire ship was displaced and scoured into the sand even further. The power of that swell must have been amazing." Wow.

12

Arundo

GPS: 40°10.69 / 73°40.12
LORAN: 26796 / 43523
Distance: 17.3 miles northeast from Manasquan Inlet, 15.3 miles east from Shark River Inlet
Depth: 80 to 130 feet
Target Species: Mako, Thresher sharks, Giant Bluefin Tuna, Cod, Pollock, Sea Bass
Prime Time of Year: June, early July (SHK), September October (GBT), November through February (COD, POL, CON)

In a particularly turbulent week in late April during WWII, German subs sunk a host of vessels, and on April 28, 1942, the 412-foot *Arundo* became a casualty. A torpedo launched from German submarine *U-136* ripped her open and sent her down, while she carried a cargo of two steam locomotives, 123 trucks and jeeps and various other cargo for the war effort. Six crewmembers were killed in the attack, and the remnants settled to the bottom of the Mud Hole.

Over the last 60 years, the *Arundo* has rested in the upper western reaches of the Mud Hole, sitting in 120 to 130 feet of water. According to Captain Steve Nagiewicz of the *Diversion II*, "The site is scattered in a 300 to 400 foot area and resembles your neighbor's backyard with junk all over the place, including Jeep tires and hundreds of Molson beer bottles. It's pretty blown up, with scraps of the wreck everywhere."

Nagiewicz has been able to see things under the water that we fishermen only see as red blobs on our fishfinders. He states, "You can still see the rusting remains of the two steam locomotives, one of which is located in her aftermost hold buried in debris, while the other is lying on its side in the sand. There are also remains of heavy iron including wheels and boilers showing on railroad cars. You can see all varieties of fish hanging and feeding on the downtide sides of the wreckage, so if I could give any advice, it'd be to fish the downtide side when anchored on her."

The highest point of the wreck is the stern area, which sits 40 to 50 feet off the bottom, and the entire wreck lays in mud more

The Giants of the Atlantic, giant bluefin tuna course through Jersey's waters, especially the Mud Hole area

than sandy bottom. The Arundo is plied year-round by the party boat packet, and it is targeted by the charter boat faction pretty heavily. Bluefin tuna make a habit of appearing in June and July, and in years past, when ling were abundant, the place was known as a select site to rattle it up with giant bluefin, and can still be a good bet if anglers sought after the giants as much as they did in the past. In June and early July, small to medium makos of 100 to 175 pounds will show up in the slick when sharking, but inshore shark species such as threshers and duskies are more apt to hit the mackerel and bluefish baits. During winter the place becomes a haven for bottom dwellers. Red hake, purple hake, sea bass, cod, and pollock will gravitate around the wreckage. You'll also find some uglies hanging around, and one trip in particular during mid-January, I hooked into four of the largest radioactive-looking conger eels I have ever seen, eels between 15 and 30 pounds and 4 to 6 feet long! There's always something going on at the *Arundo*, and you can plug it in for anything from handfuls of ling, to 700 pound giant bluefin tuna.

HOT SHOT TIP
Try this spot for the Giants in the fall. Period.

13

Klondike

GPS: 40'08.95 / 73'54.56
LORAN: 26899 / 43518
Distance: 5.5 miles northeast out of Manasquan Inlet
Depth: 46 to 80 feet
Target Species: Sea Bass, Fluke, Bonito
Prime Time of Year: June through October (SEB, FLK), October (BON)

Eureka! I've struck it rich! Those are not exactly, but most probably, the words that the first commercial boaters burst out with when they loaded up on huge catches at the Klondike. It has been suggested that the Klondike got its famous name during the great Gold Rush. While the miners of the Alaskan Klondike were getting gold fever, New Jersey dory fishermen were harvesting gold of a fishy nature. Our Klondike can't be mined for gold, but it sure can be mined for a variety of gamefish.

The Klondike is comprised of a heterogeneous mixture of bottom structure. Mainly, the area is comprised of natural, porous rock that was formed by the hardening of clay 10,000 years ago. Sandstone anchors the area as well and sometimes you will hook into a piece that will stick to your hook and come up to the surface. The area is dotted by clusters of rockpiles and semi-hard mats of mussel beds, with water depths running 46 feet on the north side to 80 feet on the east side. The underwater ridge runs east to west with a slightly north pull and is about one mile long. And in a stroke of good fortune, in recent years a barge filled with rocks and boulders intended for the Sea Girt reef missed its drop point and inadvertently spilled its load over the inshore half of the Klondike area.

HOT SHOT TIP
Drift near the outskirts of the spilled rockpiles with 3 to 5-inch squid strips to hang a citation sized sea bass.

The Klondike is renowned as a party-boat hot spot, and if the captains of the party boat fleet put their faith in it, you should too. Captain Willie Egerter of the *Dauntless* relies on the Klondike to put up some serious bag limits during his peak party boat months. "Summertime and fall, we concentrate on the numerous amounts of black sea bass that inhabit the area. It's a steady pull of keeper sea bass over 12 inches, as well as some real humpbacks that push the 5-pound mark." But it's not all about sea bass. Serious sized fluke hang all over the slopes of the Klondike. Captain Bob Bogan of the *Gambler* adds, "From the middle of May thru October we actively target large fluke. There's usually plenty of 17-inch-plus fluke to take home for dinner as well as a nice selection of 4 to 7 pounders that come up here. And that all happens until water gets cold from a south blow and the spiny dogfish move in, then all bets are off." During August and September, incidental bluefish are caught over the slopes, and it was only a decade or so ago that bonito ran rampant during October for those drifting smelts and bucktails. If the cycle hits again, it may change and bonito may make a comeback to the Klondike. Bogan states that in recent years a healthy population of squid have held there in numbers, and his fares have been jigging up livies to send them back down for doormat fluke. But the real trick to the spot? Bobby Bogan advises, "Feel it out. Let your drift go down the slope into the 60 to 65 foot range on either side north or south, and work the edges hard. The biggest mistake is giving up on a drift and picking up too early. Let the drift take you into the deeper water down the slopes into the mid-60 foot range."

14

Sea Girt Reef

GPS: 40'07.60 / 73'56.70
LORAN: 26910 / 43504
Distance: 3.5 miles east/northeast of Manasquan Inlet, 4.3 miles southeast from Shark River Inlet
Depth: 57 to 75 feet
Target Species: Sea Bass, Porgy, Triggerfish, Blackfish, Fluke, Little Tunny
Prime Time of Year: April through December (SEB, BLK)—May through October (FLK, POR, LTY, TRG)

Possibly the greatest asset to the casual daytime saltwater angler comes to be described easily in three words–Sea Girt Reef. At a manageable distance from the two major inlets of Manasquan and Shark River, this man-made reef is probably the most angler-friendly and accessible of all Jersey's reef sites. You can call it the politician's reef: it tries to please everybody. It's a bottom fishing bonanza here. What makes this place so special is that it can be fished easily for a family day out or plied with targeted precision for trophy bottom dwellers.

This reef is from the old school in Jersey, and with the deteriation of the older vessels that make up parts of the reef, it has continually been added to over the years. The reef site runs from northeast to south with a bend in the elbow about midway through, and the total area encompasses 1.3 square miles. A wild variety of structure exists on the reef that fish can call home. A total of 14 barges, three commercial vessels, seven tugboats, a plethora of army tanks, half of a tanker, a dry dock and literally tons of concrete rubble accentuate the bottom contour. Some worthwhile lengths to hit include a 100-foot dry dock, a 270-foot barge, a 242-foot tanker sponsored by *The Fisherman Magazine*, the *Carlson III*, a 70-foot clam boat, the 205-foot ferry, *Cranford*, a 75-foot trawler, the *Kiley B*, and a 95-foot tug dubbed the *Rockland County*. Water depths range from 57 feet on the western portions to 75 feet on the eastern edges of the reef.

HOT SHOT TIP

To maximize your time for variety of species, use a high-lo rig, with two dropper loops spaced 16 inches apart fixed with 3/0 baitholder hooks and squid or clams for bait.

So what's on tap? To put it mildly, a little bit from all ends of the saltwater spectrum. It's a perfect cross section of inshore Jersey fish. Your best bet is to hit the reef anywhere from May through October, the pinnacle of the summer season, where an eclectic summertime variety of sea bass, fluke, triggerfish, bluefish, porgies and blackfish will hook themselves. Most abundant during the sunny, warm days of late spring through early fall, sea bass bring a mess of attention to reef anglers. Porgies to 2 pounds will inhabit the area biting clam strips during midsummer. Recent years have brought back the triggerfish, pecking away at small clam and squid bits. Bluefish maraud through during summer months, but make no mistake, with quality gamefish come the less desirable fish. Inevitably, you will get your poundings from sea robins, skates, and smooth dogfish. Fluke tend to take up residence and grow big here. It's normally a keeper-size site for flatties, but every now and then if you set up and hit the sides of the wrecks or edges of the bridge rubble, look out, you'll be linked up with a doormat fluke over 10 pounds. And on the subject of variety, for the record, literally, the New Jersey state and world-record Gray Tilefish was taken here, weighing 10 pounds 9 ounces caught in 2001 by Jim Zigarelli. The beauty of the Sea Girt reef lies in its ability to produce quantity and diversity of fish. This place is liquid gold and has bailed me out more than once when I needed to impress a girlfriend with my fish-catching abilities. One after another, a bluefish, a sea bass, a fluke—it'll make you look like you know what you're doing. This is also a spot for the leisure fisherman who just wants to take a load off. I've spent countless hours on Sea Girt, drifting with a beverage in hand and rod in the other on a sunny summer day, bouncing for whatever hits, taking the day in.

15

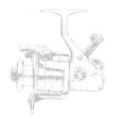

Glory Hole

GPS: 39'56.35 / 73'16.80
LORAN: 26580 / 43367
Distance: 36 miles east/southeast from Manasquan Inlet, 38 miles east/northeast of Barnegat Inlet
Depth: 112 to 260 feet
Target Species: Sharks, Bluefin Tuna, Dolphin
Prime Time of Year: June to early July (SHK), July through early October (BFT, DPH)

It's not called the Glory Hole for nothing. This piece of prime mid-offshore real estate has brought some serious mako, blue and thresher shark catches over the decades, and it continues to produce. Depending on whether you depart from Manasquan or Barnegat Inlet in the northern part of the state, the ride is roughly 33 to 45 miles offshore. The Glory Hole is shaped like an underwater drainage delta, which, in essence, it was for the prehistoric Hudson River a couple of million years ago. It's got the kinds of great edges and valleys that pelagics love. In the deepest trough, the

High voltage dolphin slam headfirst into trolled lures, exploding in and out of the water when hooked.

hole runs to a depth of 260 feet near the southerly reach and rises to a plateau of 120 feet on the edges of the hole itself. A one to three hour ride will put you in water that averages 180 feet, but ranges from 25 fathoms along edges to 42 fathoms at the deepest point on the eastern end.

The prime draw here revolves around sharks. Mako sharks bully their way through the area from mid-June and patrol on through the summer, and a fat, stinky chum slick will attract these predators to your boat. The action is always on for something, and if the makos haven't taken up residence on your day out, you're pretty much guaranteed to bring in a mess of blue sharks or a thresher in with the slick. In this general area, two Jersey state shark records have been taken: Albert Jewitt's 366-pound blue shark in 1996, and Walter Tharaca's 365-pound hammerhead shark in 1985.

Not to be overlooked by any means is the high-octane bluefin tuna and dolphin bite that explodes during July through September. Captain Bob Konz of the *A-Lure* elaborates, "We regularly troll small blue and white feathers between

5.5 and 7 knots around the lobster pots and edges of the Glory
Hole. Usually it's bluefin tuna from 15 to 70 pounds and dolphin from 3 to 15 pounds, and there's a lot of activity." He's not
kidding either. In 2004 I hit the Glory Hole with Bob
Przewoznik on the *Sweet Marie* and we pounded over 30
schoolie bluefin trolling between lobster pots. Most were
between 23 and 29 inches long, and just about every boat out
there had similar results in mid-July.

For sharking, Captain Konz recommends, "Don't look
where everyone else is setting up. There's plenty of change in
bottom contour, and a five-foot change is more than enough to
set up on. We've won three shark tournaments at the Glory
Hole, and have found a nice rut that dips to 280 feet with a sharp
rise. You can find it if you look hard enough." Fair enough.

There's a ton of electricity going on at the Glory. Once
the waters hit around 64 degrees, call in sick to work, gas up
the boat, and get ready to earn your Glory.

HOT SHOT TIP
The northern edge of the Glory Hole holds the most dramatic
dropoff. Troll spreader bars and feathers for tuna here, or set up a
shark drift going northwest to southeast.

16

Bacardi

GPS: 39'52.70 / 72'39.00
LORAN: 26308 / 43310
Distance: 66 miles east of Manasquan Inlet
Depth: 180 to 190 feet
Target Species: Giant Bluefin Tuna, Tiger, Mako, Blue Sharks, Cod, Pollock
Prime Time of Year: June, October (GBT), July/August (SHK),
   August to January (POL, COD)

With a hot spot so sweet a name as the Bacardi, you can rest assured there's going to be good times had. The Bacardi wreck is officially known as the wreck of the *Durley Chine*, but as the story goes, it received its more flavorful name when some sportfisher slugged down a fast one and marked the spot with an empty Bacardi bottle. The wreck comprises one third of a lethal triangle of three nearby wrecks, the other two being the *Texas Tower* and the *Bidevind*.

Originally, the 279-foot freighter provided great structure when it sank in 1917, and used to stretch its reach from 12 to 15 feet up off the bottom, but over the last century, time and tide has deteriorated the wreck and hammered down its reach to three to five feet off the bottom in 180 feet of water, with a debris field spread out for about 300 yards. But don't worry about the condition of the wreck; like a good bar, it keeps 'em coming back.

In the 80s and early 90s, the Bacardi was most famous for a solid giant bluefin tuna bite, and still is. Captain Bob Konz of the *A-Lure* relays, that "By the first of June, we start a spring-time troll for the Giants as they migrate up the east coast through the 50 fathom line. I'll set out spreader bars rigged with 6 to 8 fresh mackerel and troll at minimum of four knots. If I'm pulling artificials, I'll bump up the speed to 6 knots." The end of September and the month of October also sees a run of bluefin tuna moving through and can average between 40 to 60 pounds, but dependent on the year class and migratory pattern, can also school up in the 100 to 250 pound class. In the last few years the Bacardi has begun to dish out the shots it's so famous for. Bluefin tuna have been congregating around the under-water wreck once again and the chunk bite on butterfish and sardines has also been a draw for the bluefin. Since it lies north-westward within 20 or so miles from the Hudson Canyon, yellowfin tuna in the 40 to 100 pound class also frequent the area.

HOT SHOT TIP

Bring 12 to 16-ounce Viking or Crippled Herring jigs, tie them with a Palomar knot on a 4-foot, 60-pound fluorocarbon leader, and two feet up tie a dropper loop to affix a 4/0 teaser. Jig 15 to 30 feet above the wreck for pollock and bluefin.

Most wrecks usually only get the notoriety of the glamour species. The bottom-fishing connoisseur knows different. Captain Bob considers the Bacardi one of the finest wrecks off the Jersey coast to target big time bruiser bottom fish named pollock. "By the second week of August to November 1, we're dropping 12 to 20 ounce Vike jigs all over that wreck, as well as rigging 6-inch squids on hi-lo rigs with 4/0 baitholder hooks to take pollock. We slam 'em there, and in the late 90s, I remember, we tied into a catch of over 300 pollock in the 15 to 18 pound class in October. Don't print that . . . Ah, print it anyway, people should know about it." On one particular trip, Captain Konz' crew started to bang out a serious pollock bite at 4 A.M. in October, when all of a sudden, the line went limp for a second on one of the reels, and then, without stopping, headed out to sea as the last of the line snapped off the reel. Giant Bluefin.

17

Manasquan Ridge

GPS: 40°01.74 / 73°56.01
LORAN: 26890 / 43445
Distance: 6.3 miles southeast of Manasquan Inlet
Depth: 48 to 75 feet
Target Species: Fluke / Bluefish / Bonito, Little Tunny
Prime Time of Year: May/June (FL), July/August (BLF), September/
October (BON, LT)

E very time I hear the words Manasquan Ridge, images of doormat fluke, alligator bluefish and even more dark and devious denizens of the deep saturate my mind. Case in point: on a late June day in 2002, I dropped down a 4-ounce chartreuse bucktail and 10-inch chartreuse split tail Mario squid strip in an effort to conjure up a fluke of barn door proportions. The drift was swift and it was tough to hold bottom with 4 ounces, thus, my bucktail waved about 20 feet off the bottom as I swung it in broad sweeping strokes. BOOM! A hit. But, interestingly, my line went slack on a Penn 965. Why? Did I lose the lure? Cut off by a bluefish? As I reeled in enough line fast enough to catch up on all the slack, I felt a thumping vibration on the end of the line. Once I clumped on about 50 yards of line, I finally caught up to that vibration. Off the port stern, a 100-pound thresher shark launched a good six feet clean out of the water, with a chartreuse bucktail dangling from its mouth. It whipped its massive tail, sounded, and absolutely liquidated 300 yards of line off my spool before we could get the engine started to chase it down. That was four and a half miles off the beach.

Okay, thresher sharks aren't the norm out on the Manasquan Ridge, but then again, maybe they are. Point is, 6.3 miles southeast of the Manasquan Inlet lays the Ridge, a half-mile hump that spans in depth from 48 feet to 75 feet. The elongated high bottom area is far enough offshore to hold the larger breeds of fluke and bluefish. May and June are the prime months to score a fluke, especially a doormat-size fluke, as the larger breeders move in from their wintering grounds offshore and make the stop on the Ridge to feed. Come September and early October, when the flounder return to their wintering grounds offshore, they once again check their bags in at the Ridge. You'll take plenty of keeper-sized fluke in the 17 to 19-inch class here, and it also has been proven to put 20-inch-plus flatties with astounding consistency in the box. Generally, you can bet on grabbing a few 3 to 5 pounders every time out if you bounce correctly for them. A fishfinder rig with a four foot, 30-pound fluorocarbon leader, and a 4/0 Gamakatsu Octopus hook lanced a quarter inch down on a seven to ten-inch strip bait of squid, sundial, sea robin or dogfish will guarantee you a tussle with a large flatfish.

But don't count out the blues. Capt. Wayne Bushnell of the *Northstar* hits the spot regularly for fluke, but concentrates on bluefish for his charters during the summer months. Bushnell says, "Find the high spots in the 48 to 53 foot range and anchor up with a chum slick to bring the choppers to the boat. Chunk with bunker or butterfish and use wire leaders on

6/0 hooks." The nighttime is the right time in summertime at the ridge for blues, and it's usually a parking lot out there during the peak season. Watch for the lights of the party boat fleet if you need help in finding direction.

For some, it's all about speed. The fall starts to bring in the speedsters of the area with bonito and little tunny running through, inhaling spearing and other small baits. Bushnell likes to troll Clark spoons of sizes 00 to 01 on a three-foot leader with drails over the ridge ends on the north side where the depth rises into the low 50-foot range. A fast six to seven knot pace will spark the speedsters. The early morning bite is best here, and the action usually shuts off before 10:00 A.M., so basically if you want a shot at some drag-peeling action, set that alarm, man, and get there early!

HOT SHOT TIP

On a fishfinder slide rig, drop a whole 10 inch squid or strip bait down to the bottom stuck on a sliding tandem hook rig. Trophy fluke will hang themselves on it.

18

Mohawk

GPS: 40°01.42 / 73°54.27
LORAN: 26877 / 43439
Distance: 7.7 miles south of Manasquan Inlet
Depth: 65 to 81 feet
Target Species: Sea bass, Fluke, Blackfish
Prime Time of Year: May through October (SEB, FLK) March, April (BLK)

Another of New Jersey's unfortunate coastwide wrecks luckily turns around to benefit recreational fishermen—the *Mohawk* wreck. On January 25, 1935 the 387-foot *Mohawk* with a crew of 109, lost its automatic steering capabilities due to mechanical malfunction and rammed into the Norwegian freighter *Talisman*. Forty-six lives were lost in the incident. Originally, when it went down, the masts stuck clear out of the water, but when the Navy found out and tracked a German U-boat that was using the *Mohawk* for a hiding spot, it was time to send the wreck down deep. The wreckage was dynamited with 16,200 pounds of explosives and then wire-dragged, so it now rises up to a depth of only 15 feet off the ocean bottom. Laying 7.7 miles from Manasquan Inlet and 11.3 miles from Shark River inlet, the remains of the *Mohawk* have for the most part become scattered and spread out, in depths that reach 81 feet of water. The entire area of the remaining debris field lies 5 miles off the shoreline and stretches in a one-eighth mile square area, and generally lay in a northeast to southwest direction, with the big, fish-attracting boilers still intact.

HOT SHOT TIP

Avoid the use of skirts and spinners when bottom bouncing the wreck. They will attract dogfish on every drop. Stick to simple, unglamorous rigs.

Actually, you couldn't ask for a better-placed wreck site, as the *Mohawk* cuts straight through the middle of three incredibly hot spots. The ruins are surrounded by the Manasquan Ridge on north side, Southeast Lump on southeast side, and East Lump off of the east side. Captain Bob Bogan of the *Gambler* lays it out like this: "The expanse of the Mohawk is extensive. You can spend a whole day shifting around on all the various piles of the wreck and get your money's worth. Get ahead of the wreck and drift through. Some chunks, like the bow section, still rise to 15 feet off the bottom, and there's always a good selection of sea bass and ling there." But with the desired fish, come the undesirables to boot. Dogfish and bergalls are all over the area and on a particularly infested day, you'll have to wade through a mess of them. The close proximity to the coast can make the spot a parking lot of sport fishermen and dive boats, especially during the summer months. But if you want to attack the spot before the crowds get there, Bogan offers some select advice—"Many people don't know it, but it's a fantastic blackfishing spot in late March through April as they move back into the inshore waters. Once the water temps hit 42 degrees, the blackfish begin the bite."

Another odd point to note here is that if you do hook into what appears to be some sort of container, don't open it, throw it back. Captain Bob relays that old time party boat captain, Captain Joe Burns, wished to be cremated and dropped on the wreck of the *Mohawk*, with a can of Budweiser fixed tight to the urn. Let Captain Burns enjoy his eternal beer and rest in peace!

19

Seaside Lump

GPS: 39'55.39 / 73'54.33
LORAN: 26864 / 43378
Distance: 12 miles southeast out of Manasquan Inlet
Depth: 54 to 85 feet
Target Species: Fluke, Bluefish
Prime Time of Year: July through September (FLK, BLF)

Surely, there's a spot in every captain's logbook that they consider a bail-out spot. One that can turn a goose egg day into at least a hey-we-got-a-tug-on-the-end-of-the-line type of day. That's the Seaside Lump. Laying nine miles off the beach of Seaside Park, the Lump can be easily reached for a pleasant day on the water.

Surrounded by deep water on all sides, the Seaside Lump sits like an underwater island. In reality, the place is a small pimple that sits pointedly in the depths, a perfect little speed bump in the middle of a migratory track that will attract baitfish and thus gamefish. Sitting on the pinnacle of the hump the depth reader will hit 54 feet, but circumnavigating around, the water depth will range from 71 to 85 feet around, with the deepest ditches on the south side.

This isn't a very large piece of real estate to fish, and your success may largely be determined on the pressure it has received in the past couple of days. There are certainly more accommodating and larger lumps that are easily reached around this area, but for what the Seaside Lump lacks in bark, it makes up for in its bite.

Fluke are the mainstay of this fishery, with peak season scoring in the heat of the summer from July through

The art of bouncing chrome ball jigs has been taking fluke fishing to a new level. Austin Perilli proves what the power of the chrome can do to a flatfish.

September, as flatties sit patiently on the edges, devouring spearing and sand eel schools that cruise through. The fact that it's a little bit further offshore than the usual inshore fluke haunts means that your chances of tallying up a limit catch or three to five pound fluke is not too farfetched. Given that there is a prevailing Jersey midafternoon south summertime wind, drifting from the south to the north is the best bet to plan an attack on the Lump, as you will hit the ledge of 50 to 80 feet water on the south side, then drift over, with most of your strikes happening from drifting up the southern side and then over the top of the Lump. Why? When a prevailing southern current and wind combine, they push bait, upwell nutrients and forage up along the southern ledge where fluke lay in wait, gobbling down everything that drifts on by their greedy mouths. Once on the top of the Lump, fluke will still be planted firmly in the sand and feed as forage continues to drift right by their noses. By the time you run over the top and move to the deeper depths, it's usually time to restart the drift, as the forage now drifts over any fluke lying in the sand on the opposite side of the Lump. Best bets here include braided line for extra sensitivity and using mid-size three to four-inch strip baits on fishfinder rigs, to allow for a free-swinging motion as the bait flutters uphill on the drift.

Other species frequent the Seaside Lump. Mid-summer action on bluefish is almost a lock-in, with larger blues from eight to 15 pounds the norm. When you run around the edges outside of the hump, keep a keen eye on the screen to find the patches of bluefish working at variable depths in the water column. Be prepared with an AVA 17 to 47 jig to drop down and reel up liquid fast to hang a blue.

HOT SHOT TIP

Use braided line, a fishfinder slide, four foot piece of 25 pound fluorocarbon, 3/0 Circle hook and a big Peruvian spearing drifted on the upwelling side of the lump.

20

Texas
Tower #4

GPS: 39'47.91 / 72'40.15
LORAN: 26313 / 43267
Distance: 66 miles out of Manasquan and Barnegat Inlets
Depth: 60 to 185 feet
Target Species: Sharks, Yellowfin, Bluefin, Cod, Pollock
Prime Time of Year: Mid-June through October (SHK), July through
   October (YFT, BFT, GBT) May through January (COD, POL)

Spawned from human forti-
tude and courage and annihilated by the fury of the Atlantic,
the wreckage of the Texas Tower now rests in its grave at the
bottom of the ocean. The Texas Tower #4 was originally a mil-
itary warning station built to withstand 125 mph winds and
waves up to 60 feet high, though the Atlantic battered away at
the tower and weakened the foundation in the mud bottom
upon which it rested. The constant battle against the elements
to repair and reinforce the tower earned it the nickname, "Old
Shaky," and eventually a crew of 28 men was dispatched to
remain on through the winter of 1960 to fortify the tower. On

January 15, 1961, in the wake of another monster winter storm, a distress signal was sent out as the tower began falling apart in the pounding sea. But even as a Coast Guard rescue ship was sent out through tumultuous seas to save the workers on the tower, the area where Texas Tower #4 was became blank on the radar screen.

The Tower now lies in 185 feet of water, very close to the 40 and 50-fathom lines, and roughly 66 miles out of the Manasquan and Barnegat inlets. The wreckage consists of radar domes, three huge support beams, and a helicopter landing pad. The Texas Tower rests at a 45-degree angle, and used to rise within 60 feet of the surface, but seems to have collapsed even further in recent years. Renowned divemaster Captain Steve Nagiewicz notes of the wreckage, "The tower structure which was originally at 60 to 70 feet has collapsed over the 1999–2000 seasons and wreckage now starts at a depth of 120 feet and is collapsing quickly."

Talk about being amped up! What could be better than landing a 150-pound class bluefin? High-fives all around!

Resting just 12 miles northwest of the Hudson Canyon's tip, the Texas Tower provides a bountiful array of underwater structure that attracts a span of species, from bottom dwellers to pelagics. Capt. Bob Balewicz of the *Carcharodon* chases tuna, sharks, cod and pollock in and around the wreckage. "When I'm making my early season exploratory canyon troll to the Hudson Canyon, I'll stop over the Texas Tower to drop very large metal jigs on it. You can actually 'feel' the jig hit the top of the Tower. Many times we've jigged good-sized yellowfin and bluefin tuna of 60 to 80 pounds here, but also some solid 15 to 20 pound pollock and cod on this little detour. It's tough to stay right on top of her, so you'll end up leaving your engines running, tracking your drift very tightly on your GPS and making drift after drift to find the depth the fish are holding at. We've had double digit catches many times while doing this."

HOT SHOT TIP

A notable point of the surrounding area is that four sunken barges are to be found within 600 yards from it on east, south and west sides in a U formation, providing even more fish-attracting structure.

The variety of fish stack and hold at different depths on the tower debris, with sea bass claiming the bottom, cod and pollock about 20 to 50 feet up, then tuna and sharks above them.

Captain Balewicz describes this bounty as "a veritable 'bait store' swimming around the Texas Tower. From the second week of June through August, I have had excellent success pulling mako and blue sharks from around the rubble, and July through October, we'll hit it for yellowfin and bluefin, sometimes even giant bluefin. Many times I've veered over in that direction, just for a look-see, and a commercial captain will call me in on the Giants. I've seen Giants pushing and splashing in the vicinity so many times that on an average outing to the Hudson, you're drawn to the Tower just to see if anything's happening."

Prevailing strong currents around the Tower means you can only get away with 20-minute drifts on shark excursions, so it's best to set up a half-mile past the Tower on a drift. More important than pinpointing a drift over the wreckage is paying more attention to the rise where the tower sits, and work the ledge that it was built upon. If you anchor up to bounce some jigs for tuna or cod, mind the structure, as anchor lines can be severed instantly by the sharp, rusted remnants.

21

Tolten Lump

GPS: 39'51.60 / 73'48.40
LORAN: 26813 / 43336
Distance: 19 miles from both Manasquan and Barnegat Inlets
Depth: 49 to 85 feet
Target Species: Bluefish, Bonito, Small Mako Sharks
Prime Time of Year: June through October (BLF and SHK),
July through September (BON)

Named for the nearby shipwreck of the *Tolten*, the Tolten Lump provides an attractive hideout in the middle of flat bottom for many pelagic species. The sandy bottom bulge is a pretty defined squared knoll that lies along the 15-fathom line and runs in a direction a little bit north to south. It contains depths of generally 55 feet on the point to 85 feet off the sides, and covers a small piece of about a half-mile square. It may be a small piece, but it's got a lot of punch.

The small size is still enough to create conditions of upwelling in the area, pushing nutrients upward from the seafloor, drawing sand eels and spearing to chow down on the nutrients and copepods. Since it's far enough offshore and butts up against the 15-fathom line, you can bet on a whole array of pelagics milling around the area. Captain Bob Bogan of the *Gambler* will regularly hit this area for bluefish on the night trips. "June through October, Tolten Lump is a bluefish frenzy. We anchor up with one anchor and chum all night long. Usually we'll find blues in the four to twelve pound class, with larger ones moving through, and lots of times we read them right on the bottom of the lump. Though a lot of guys drift their chunks out, there's better way. Take a dropper rig with a bank sinker on the bottom and 18 inches up, tie a dropper with a six inch steel leader with a 5/0 hook. Drop down and crank one to two cranks right off the bottom, using smelt, bunker backs or butterfish for bait. They'll whack it immediately, and you'll outfish the other guys two to one." And the bluefishing isn't limited to a night bite; daytime jiggers can also produce when drifting over the lump.

HOT SHOT TIP
For a bonito rig, use a 5-foot shot of 12-pound test fluorocarbon leader and snell on a 1/0 to 2/0 bonito hook using a well-hidden smelt or spearing, hooked through the mouth and under the gill.

Bluefish aren't the only residents—come August bonito to six or seven pounds will motor through the area. Chum with cut up and whole spearing, and drop down a whole spearing to hook into a speedster. You can troll over the lump at a fast six-knot pace with #2 or #4 Clark spoons or small feathers in Green/Yellow combinations to attract the bonito. With the influx of bluefish and bonito in the late summer and early fall, small mako sharks find their way to stake out the unsuspecting fish. There's potential here to tie into four or five small makos in the 50 to 70-pound class during a day out, as they sit tight near the lump to feed on the bluefish. This can be an exciting time, dispersing bunker chunks out to fight some bluefish, then filleting a bluefish and sending it out on a white skirt at a mid-range depth of 20 to 40 feet or flatlined out the back. It's a fun light tackle spot for makos, and you need to make short drifts over the area. Do not overlook this spot for a chance to fight a small mako, as it's worthwhile to set up for them.

22

Chicken Canyon

GPS: 39'47.00 / 72.59.19
LORAN: 26450 / 43275
Distance: 45 to 55 miles from Barnegat and Manasquan Inlets
Depth: 168 feet to 248 feet
Target Species: Yellowfin, Bluefin, Bigeye, Sharks, Dolphin
Prime Time of Year: July through October (YFT, BFT, BET) June,
early July (SHK), July through October, (DPH)

There are two stories behind the origin of the name Chicken Canyon. One–from the ever-present amount of chickbirds that are there anytime and every time you hit the spot, and two–that the spot is three-quarters of the way to the Hudson Canyon, and if you didn't make it quite all the way out to the Hudson, and stopped at this spot instead, you were chicken. Pick whichever fable you want, the Chicken Canyon will still remain as a red-hot shark, tuna and dolphin spot.

The Chicken Canyon, a 15 mile-long region, is dug almost at the end of the drainage delta of the prehistoric

Hudson River channel, laying in the eastward side of the end of the Mud Hole, and acts as the middleman between the Glory Hole and the Hudson Canyon. The expanse is a big depression that hits 42 fathoms, but the valley is circled by shallower depths of 30 to 35 fathoms. Captain Pete Barrett of the *Linda B* considers the Chicken a great daytime spot for the average boat fisherman. "The Chicken Canyon is an area where yellowfin and bluefin tuna will spill out of the Hudson and come up out of 500 feet plus water and spread out to follow the warm water onto the flats. A fantastic way to target this spot is to stick to the southern wall where the edge goes from 26 to 42 fathoms in a 3-mile range. It's a more severe, immediate drop, as compared to the north side which is a more gentle sloping area."

Bluefin tuna from "popeye" size of 10 to 15 pounds to schoolies of 20 to 30 pounds to giant bluefin inhabit the area, mostly from mid-June and then from mid-August until October, depending upon the path of the regional

For maximum control, tuna should be gaffed in the head area if possible, as they are easier to maneuver and will not explode with the power of their tail and take off with your gaff. You'll also get more steaks out of 'em.

baitfish and their habits. Trolling four-inch Huntington Drone spoons or Clark spoons with one-ounce egg sinkers wired to their noses will score the bluefin, but when yellowfin are around, medium to large ballyhoo rigged with split-bills and broken backs and Green Machines will bring them up into the spread. Barrett notes, "Troll in a stitching pattern from wall to wall, over the canyon, sewing the sides together. This way, you cover the edges of both walls, and the valley between. If you do get into tuna, stay on that spot, because even though they'll usually move a few hundred yards around, they will stay put in that area for some time. Chances are something is holding them there, such as bait or warmer water."

HOT SHOT TIP

Bring 4 to 5 inch, fresh, tapered hickory shad, mackerel or herring strips to lance on your bucktails and cast around the lobster pots for dolphin.

One of the most explosive acts to hit the scene at the Chicken Canyon is the population of dolphin. Mahi-mahi from grasshoppers (1 to 3 pounds), to pugnacious bulls of 30 to 40 pound plus will butt heads with you. The place is littered with lobster pots, and the dolphin stick tight around them. Captain Pete recommends, "If you're trolling for the dolphin, always put the pot between you and the sun, keeping your shadow off of them. If they see your shadow, they'll spook and dive down deeper. Once you stop getting strikes on the troll, make no mistake, they're still around. Pull in the troll lines and start drifting by the pots, casting bucktails or small chunks of butterfish to them. You'll find that they didn't leave the area, they just moved lower in the water column." And not only dolphin consider the pots of the Chicken Canyon the place to be. On a flat calm day on one of Barrett's trips, he and his crew were trolling by a pot and noticed a bill protruding from the surface. They dropped back a medium ballyhoo back to it and immediately got hamhocked by a 250-pound blue marlin on gear set up for 15-pound dolphin. They landed it.

23

 **Barnegat Light Reef**

GPS: 39'45.30 / 74'01.50
LORAN: 26892 / 43277
Distance: 3.1 miles east from Barnegat Inlet
Depth: 46 to 63 feet
Target Species: Fluke, Sea Bass, Porgies
Prime Time of Year: June through September (FLK, SEB)

I struggled with how to approach this one for two reasons. One, because it's so productive, as the entire Barnegat Light Reef is incredible with an area spanning .85 square miles and dimensions of 1.75 miles north to south and three-quarters mile wide. It contains tons of tanks, bunches of reef balls, concrete castings, and low profile structure, including wrecks like a 40-foot crew barge, the 41-foot sailboat *Antares*, and 42-foot tuna barge, all of which is easily fish and angler friendly. This brings me to reason two–because I consider this one of my favorite fluke spots, and I was feeling selfish. But duty prevailed.

This reef has been responsible for a flabbergasting amount of fluke in the 3 to 14-pound range in the last few years. I'm talking about day in and day out catches weighing in at shops such as Mike Haluska's Mole's Bait and Tackle, where Haluska would see at least a dozen fluke come through the door during the late summer months almost every single day, all between 5 and 12 pounds. This is a drift fisherman's reef, with a variety of low-lying snags and hang-ups to drift over for fluke.

Most anglers out for a day of drift fishing for fluke will try to start their drifts at the north end and gradually move south over the site. With a prevailing south wind in the afternoon and evening, the early morning and noontime hours are the best bet to get that special drift. When the south wind kicks in after noon, the cooler water gets pushed up the coastline and the reef is close enough to shore for the fish to feel the effects; in other words, they shut their mouths when the cooler water pushing through hits them. One big, hour-long drift in the morning will usually will put a stack of flatties into the boat, and the outgoing tide produces best, as nutrients and forage outflow from nearby Barnegat Inlet into the ocean waters sticking to the reef.

HOT SHOT TIP

If the drift is running too fast to hold bottom, throw a sea anchor out to slow you down, in order to effectively spend some time by the assorted low-profile structure.

You'll cover ground that ranges from 46 to 58 feet of water for the most part, and the right recipe for success is to be feeling the bottom when you bounce between the various patches of tire units, tanks and concrete rubble. Fluke will be sticking close to the little underwater refuges and will pounce on your offering as it wafts by in the current. June through

August will dial you in to prime time season. If you are inclined to experience the excellent sea bassing as well, you can drop down with clam baits to hang humpbacks that will exceed 6 pounds here. Blue-dyed squid strips are a good bet to use for sea bass to boot. Pay attention as well to the cluster of tanks that are submerged on the southwest side, as it's a virtual city for sea bass.

24

Resor
Wreck

GPS: 39'46.65 / 73'25.30
LORAN: 26638 / 43277
Distance: 31.7 miles east/southeast from Barnegat inlet, 34.4 miles
  southeast from Manasquan Inlet
Depth: 57 feet to 125 feet
Target Species: Sharks, Cod, Pollock
Prime Time of Year: June July (SHK), November December (COD, POL)

One of the most notable casualties of the World War II German sub wolfpack was the unfortunate sinking of the 435-foot Standard Oil Company tanker, *R.P. Resor*. German sub *U-578* intercepted and torpedoed the *Resor* on February 26, 1942 and all but two of the 43-man crew perished. The *U-578* was tracked down in the waters off of Spain and was vengefully sunk by Allied bombers.

Nowadays, sharks of another breed hang around the wreckage. The Resor is probably most notorious for the shark fishing opportunity that presents itself here. The wreck generally lies in an average of 125 feet of water and is scattered over

400 feet on a hard sand bottom. Lying northeast to southwest, the highest point reaching a height of 40 feet up is the stern section, which is interestingly enough rooted by the 3-inch deck gun which, when sinking, penetrated into the sand and anchored itself like a fencepost! Steel beams, sheets of metal and twisted debris litter the wreckage area, detailing the extensive torpedo damage above. The two highest peaks are the wheel-house and bow, and the stern, both of which are separated by 300 feet of hard sand bottom. The bottom growth of the whole ground area hosts clam beds and kelp patties, attracting a wide range of species to the wreck to forage on the fertile grounds.

Expansive schools of Atlantic mackerel and bluefish course along the 20-fathom line through the area during the late spring and early summer, attracting an array of sharks, which include mako, thresher, blue, and Great white sharks. Most tournament anglers plug in the *Resor* for their first choice

Snaggle-toothed mako sharks make spectacular, acrobatic leaps when hooked, and sometimes, makos have been known to jump right into the cockpit. Bernie Walker and the author take this mako home to the grill.

in tangling with a shark. Captain Bob Konz of the *A-Lure*, considers this a high-energy sharking spot. "You've got about 57 to 63 feet of water above the wreck, which gives a good profile for sharks to cruise in, out and around. I find that a good area to work is when the depth finder hits 92 feet. There's an area of fingers just south that corrals mackerel schools in the early summer as they follow the 20-fathom line. Sharks are right on them." The shark season is hottest here during June and early July, but at times there can be some pretty thick crowds working the wreck, especially during tournament weekends.

HOT SHOT TIP
Before setting out your chum buckets for a shark slick, complete a 200-yard circle around the area you plan to fish, with the chum bucket draped over the side. The extra cloud of slick will get the attention of nearby sharks immediately.

But sharking isn't the only attraction. The *Resor* holds a monumental place in the book of cod fishermen. Captain Konz relays, "When we hit it right, in November and December, this place is gold for cod. We'll set up with five bushels of clams and fish the high piece. I'm tellin' ya, we bag cod of 30 and 40 pounds there regularly, one trip we bagged 109 cod from 10 to 40 pounds on the charter. It was amazing. They were hitting clams and also AVA jigs with green tubes. Green colors work the best here for some reason. We've proved that."

The cod fishing is enhanced by Pollock and monkfish, which also inhabit the area. The *Resor* offers a secret spot for dedicated bottom bouncers as well as die-hard Jaws hunters.

25

Barnegat Ridge—North and South

GPS: North 39'42.19 / 73'47.97; South 39'38.41 / 73'47.15
LORAN: North 26791 / 43240; South 26778 / 43202
Distance: 14 miles east/southeast of Barnegat Inlet
Depth: 54 to 62 feet
Target Species: Bluefish, Fluke, School Bluefin, Little Tunny, Bonito
Prime Time of Year: Late May through October (BLF), May through October (FLK), July through October (BFT, LIT, BON)

What a serious dynamic duo. Running a quick 14 miles ESE of Barnegat Inlet, you will be located in the midst one of the finest one-two punch combos that New Jersey has to offer. In tackle shops and on the charter fleets, when there's action happening, the Barnegat Ridge is usually referred from word of mouth as just that, the Barnegat Ridge, but the reality is that the Ridge is split up into two separate areas, Barnegat North and Barnegat South, and both sections have incredible, separate opportunities hidden in their distinct personae.

First off, the distance between the two ridges is just under 1.2 miles from edge to edge, and you can jump between the ridges easily to maximize bag limits, varied species, and flat-out fun. The North Ridge covers roughly a three-quarters by 2-mile elongated area that runs northeast to southwest. The shallowest point hits 54 feet on the northwest corner and the shallow area extends like a tabletop through the middle of the ridge down to the southeast corner, with two deeper gullies on each side that dip between 60 and 62 feet, and then shallower water of 56 to 58 feet on the outsides of the gullies. Picture an underwater "W" and you've nailed what the ridge looks like underwater. That's the North's layout.

In the 1.2 miles between the North and South, the water scope varies from 61 to 70 feet, and the grounds are productive. Then you hit the top of the South Ridge.

HOT SHOT TIP

NORTH RIDGE: During mid-August, bounce 2 to 6 ounce chrome balls on the tip of the "W" for fluke on one side of boat; on the other side jig metals for bluefin, bonito, skipjacks and false albacore.
SOUTH RIDGE: Anchor up and chunk spearing on the "black hole" notch on the south side of the ridge for bluefin tuna.

Overall, in total makeup, the South is shallower and a bit thinner than the North. Once again, this ridge, like its sister, runs northeast to southwest but covers a slightly smaller area of roughly one-half by 1.5 miles. The most unusual and productive nook lies on the southern end, where the depth runs from 56 to 61 to 54 feet in a cut-out notch. And most secretly, about a half-mile immediately south of the south part of the ridge, is a steep drop that plummets from 57 to 93 feet very abruptly.

Darren Dorris, saltwater editor of the *New Jersey Angler Magazine*, spells out the entire year on the Barnegat Ridges. "It begins with a mackerel fishery in April if they stay in relatively close. The Ridge catches the fluke migrating inward during May and June and they hold tight there until September comes. The summer population of fluke is astounding, as they seem to consider it a major congregating point, with larger fluke to 12 pounds sticking around for the duration. June through September is a rock-solid blue fishery of tailor sized blues from 2 to 3 pounds to true alligators to 20 pounds." But you can't forget about the diamond in the rough fishery that exists at the Ridge during the month of July. Dorris states, "School bluefin and even bluefin to 50 pounds are caught every year here in the heat of the summer. Troll cedar plugs and small feathers for them in the early morning, then chunk with tiny stuff such as spearing or sand eels during the daytime."

The months of July through October also see a battalion of bonito and little tunny running through the perimeter, especially around the edges of the drop-offs. You can work this area like magic if you do it right. Start your troll at the top of the North Ridge and continue over it in a Z-pattern all the way through the South Ridge. Clark Spoons and green or pink feathers seem to work best before 10 A.M., but many locals say that staying out later than that is a waste of time as the bite invariably comes to a halt.

Widespread, both ridges are known for the absolutely slamming bluefish action that occurs within and around their boundaries. Starting in late May through October, anglers can find intense bluefishing all around the edges of the ridges, but particularly the 11 Fathom Lump to the south of the South ridge is a red-hot point. There the water rises from a depth of 80 feet to a more shallow 55 feet. This sudden drop-off harbors marauding bluefish from 5 to 20 pounds where a messy chum slick and chunked bunker on a 7/0 baitholder hook and a six-inch steel leader hammer the blues.

There's so much going on at Barnegat Ridge, it's tough to decide what you're going to target once you're there. Oh yeah, another thing. If it makes your decision any harder for you, historically one or two white marlin and a few wahoo are caught here every year at the end of the summer. Get the outriggers ready!

26

Harvey Cedars Lump

GPS: 39'40.08 / 74'05.40
LORAN: 26907 / 43223
Distance: 6 miles southeast of Barnegat Inlet
Depth: 28 to 52 feet
Target Species: Fluke, Bluefish, Porgy, Weakfish, Croaker
Prime Time of Year: May through October (FLK, BLF, POR, WEK, CRK)

For the fishermen who fish off of Long Beach Island, there's one location that rests within a comfortable 3 miles of the beachfront—the Harvey Cedars Lump. Bearing southeast out of Barnegat Inlet, it's an easy ride to some fluke-friendly grounds, as the diminutive mound is more like a humble pile of sand stacked up in a pool of deep water. It's a relatively small pimple that is encompassed by deeper water on all sides. The tip of the pinnacle hits 28 feet and on all sides, the water recedes from 40 to 66 feet, almost immediately. This is a premier summertime spot, in that a medley of species considers it a virtual clubhouse to cut back and congregate.

Weakfish readily inhale plastic jigs, metals, sandworms, and grass shrimp. Tom Harrison drifted grass shrimp at Barnegat Inlet to put this papermouth on ice.

Sticking tight to the slopes of the hump, fluke lay in wait to chase the spearing, rainfish and crabs that meander about the slope. Most of the fluke tend to stick themselves in the deeper water from 30 feet down to 50 feet during the summertime, where they can get cool away from the heat of the sun. The southwest corner hits a bottom of 52 feet, and is a good place to search for fluke. Croakers and porgies can be found schooling above the flatties, along the hump's shoulders all through the summer as well, and a well-placed strip of squid or clam bits will take them at the depth they mark on the fishfinder.

A clutch point to bring up of the Harvey Cedars Lump is that it is situated just inside the three-mile limit for striped bass, and October and November will bring many bass to the tight little pinnacle to feed. Jigging is the preferred method at this time of year. Fall has seen a nice array of weakfish in recent years, as the sea trout regularly take smaller ½ to 1½ ounce jigs and bucktails tipped with pork rind or three to four inch plastic grub tails during September and October. Yellow and white colored grubs have been the ticket. Many times you will see the fleet of party boats hitting the Harvey Cedars Lump in the thick of the summer, where they put up a mixed catch of fluke, weakfish, and porgies for their fares. The morning bite is best on the weakfish, and late morning through afternoon ignites the fluke bite. Smaller bluefish run around like packs of wild dogs, and you can be cleaned out of plastic baits in a few hours by one to three pound blues, basically spring through fall. One problem here seems to be the infiltration of dogfish during the summer, as they will grab anything from jigs to baits intended for other species, but they also seem to hang on top of the lump in the shallower water, if that gives you any idea of what area to avoid here.

A set of two lumps that hit the 25 foot mark also occur just northwest and southwest of Harvey Cedars Lump, so if the hump doesn't produce, you can always head west a few hundred yards and cover new sloping ground in a few minutes. It's a circus of all types of finned fare here, and though nothing of any real size frequents the area, there can be lot of action on any given day.

HOT SHOT TIP
Hook a killie through the lips, a 3 inch strip of squid, and a frozen spearing through the eyes for a combination to attract all sorts of species.

27

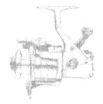

The Fingers

GPS: 39 30.10 / 73 30.00
LORAN: 26650 / 43125
Distance: 25 to 35 miles southeast from Barnegat and Manasquan Inlets
Depth: 108 to 132 feet
Target Species: Sharks, Bluefin Tuna, Yellowfin Tuna
Prime Time of Year: Mid-June, July (SHK) August to mid-September
(BFT, YFT)

Like a greedy hand, the Fingers grab pelagic species and hold them there tight. This vast-spanning spot covers an area of 75 square miles, and ranges in depth from 17 to 23 fathoms. The Fingers are a continuous series of large subterranean humps, both short and long, comprised of hard, packed sand.

Captain Pete Barrett of the *Linda B* considers the Fingers one of his mainstays for shark fishing. "In the 70s and 80s, after everybody got the 'JAWS' syndrome, shark fishing became popular and the guys from the Jersey Coast Shark Anglers really put the Fingers on the chalkboard. Each separate finger runs in a southwest to northeast fashion, and the irregular bottom will attract bait such as mackerel, squid and butterfish to its reaches. Starting at the Star mark on the northwest side, which is the mark of the compass rose on the chart, an ideal shark drift would take you from northwest to southeast over the whole area. The general flow of the current is north to south, and if you have a mild northwest wind, this would be the best way to begin targeting the spot."

HOT SHOT TIP

Barrett's shark rig consists of a wind-on 16 foot section of 300 pound leader, attached by a 300 pound class barrel swivel, to a four-foot piece of single strand wire, via haywire twist to a 8/0 to 10/0 offset #7699 hook. A green skirt is draped over a bluefish or hickory shad fillet, and a rattle is affixed just above the hook.

Shark fishermen will drift over changes in depth from eight to 15 feet over the whole area, but sometimes, conditions are not on your side. If that's the case, Barrett recommends a change in the plan of action. "Say you get a southeast wind on your day out. With the prevailing north-to-south drift on a southeast wind, you'll make a 'banana' drift in an arc. To turn a bad condition into a good one, set up on the southeast corner of the fingers, where you'll banana over a prime part of the southerly section of the fingers."

Mako, threshers, blue, dusky and tiger sharks will be the main species you will encounter here, and sometimes warm water eddies will migrate inshore and you will experience clear blue water—not canyon-clear quality, but of a very deep blue. That's when the Fingers produce the best. Bluefin and yellowfin tuna will make their presence known in August through mid-September, and most of the time, trolled daisy chains with small purple squids are money to bag a few. Dolphin, skipjacks and the occasional smaller wahoo will also add to the late summer fare. If you are out sharking and do run across some tuna, you can decide to keep the chum bucket in the water and throw the anchor to set up to chunk for them, but Barrett warns, "Chasing tuna during the shark season is like chasing rainbows. Unless you are marking them tight and often, keep on the drift, but if they are sticking around, it's worth it to set up on the chunk for them."

The Fingers, though, are best known for sharks. Captain Pete has plied some monsters from the grip of the Fingers. "The two largest sharks I've had there were a 418-pound mako and an estimated 900-pound tiger shark, but probably one of the most memorable times was when we threw out a Mako Magnet device that brought three 200 to 250-pound makos to the boat, which we caught, schools of yellowfin tuna in the 50-pound class, and then a huge whale that came smack under our boat, I mean right under it, and we were thinking, all he needed to do was lift his tail and we were goners! Luckily, he didn't."

28

Brigantine Shoal

GPS: 39'23.50 / 74'20.0
LORAN: 26960 / 43050
Distance: 1.5 miles northeast of Absecon Inlet
Depth: 6 to 56 feet
Target Species: Brown, Dusky, Sand Tiger Shark, Fluke, Weakfish, Bluefish
Prime Time of Year: August (SHK), July through September (FLK, WEK)
   May through November (BLF)

Mired in history of pirate ships and lore of the Jersey Devil, the town of Brigantine holds its fair share of monster tales. The volatile area of the Brigantine shoals that rests roughly 1.5 miles northeast of Absecon Inlet is no exception to this claim. The shoals vary greatly in their shallows and depths. The whole area is wide and encompasses an area of approximately 1.5 square miles, with its shallowest points rising to 6 feet and the valleys diving to 56 feet. This bumpy range creates upwelling and offers hiding spots for baitfish. But on the shifting tides, a washing machine effect occurs and the waters get rippy, as they shove and push the baitfish around, creating confusion for bait, which the resident predatory species find nicely accommodating. The eastern side of the shoal has the greatest variation of lumps, as some pinnacles reach 24 feet and drop down to 54 feet in an instant.

But back to the monsters of Brigantine . . . The Brigantine backwater estuaries of Absecon Bay and Great Bay, both of which are less than a two-mile trip from the shoal waters, are the breeding grounds for brown and sand tiger sharks. This means the predators have to pass directly over the Brigantine Shoals to get there. Thus, if you play your cards right, you can go toe-to-toe with some quality sharks not more than a mile off the beachfront. Brigantine surfcasters regularly tie into brown sharks right from the suds during the month of August, and Dusky sharks have also been taken right from the sands. Boat fishermen have the upper hand in August, as they can effectively draw the nearshore sharks in with a well-dispersed chum slick. A bunker chum bucket should be draped over the side to start the morning, with whole fillets of bunker or mackerel wafting in the current behind. A brown, sand tiger, or dusky shark will finish the equation for you, though all sand tigers must be released as they are a protected species.

HOT SHOT TIP
Set up on a drift, chum bucket over the side, bouncing bucktails for fluke, while sending back mackerel or bunker fillets out for sharks.

Bluefish regularly gang up in these waters year round, chasing the disoriented baitfish, and you can always spot birds working the area in summer and fall where the blues push the hapless bait to the surface while hammering them from below. Bring your topwater poppers here, such as the four-inch Stillwater Smack-It or one ounce Atom Poppers to experience heated surface action. The shoals also contribute to excellent summertime fluke and weakfish activity, and will produce stripers during the fall. Try bouncing around the area on the eastern side for large fluke, where the drop goes from 24 to 52 feet quickly. During the fall, set up on the western side of the shoal, where stripers tend push in and feed on the baitfish, many times creating blitzing conditions right outside Absecon Inlet over the thin shoals that hit seven feet. Most of the shoal region is contained within the three-mile federal limit, but when bass fishing, be wary of the demarcation line on your GPS unit.

This place can be some real fun if you know that monsters with wide dorsal fins and sharp teeth abound here. Sink a bunker fillet out there, and see what you come up with.

29

Lucy the Elephant

GPS: 74'30.29 / 39'19.00
LORAN: 42990 / 27010
Distance: 3 miles north of Great Egg Inlet
Depth: 30 to 50 feet
Target Species: Weakfish, Croakers, Bluefish, Little Tunny, Striped Bass
Prime Time of Year: August through November (WEK, CRK, LIT)
 October through December (BLF)

Like you've never seen a 65-foot tall wooden elephant on a beach before. Lucy the Elephant is an eccentric landmark standing proud along the beachfront in Margate that has captured the attention of boat anglers year round for more reasons than shock value. Her enormous gray and goofy presence not only marks the site of a historic hotel, but Lucy is a landmark to set your fishing log to. About three-quarters to one mile off Lucy, the underwater sea floor drops in stages from 35 to 50 feet. This dramatic drop attracts bait into its ledges and therefore a variety of species to the cut.

Running along the piece, stretching anywhere between one and two miles from the Great Egg bell and straight off Lucy, the fishing grounds get productive fast. A prominent 30-foot line runs north to south along the coast and sportfish stick to the gradual slope on the eastern side like Velcro. Captain Bryan Dileo of Iowa Fortune Charters considers the area a no-frills good spot. "The bottom here is a typical current-ribbed, sandy bottom, fluctuating up and down one foot in depth. This area tends to be a fish-finder spot for migrating weakfish as we slowly work the area until the marks start showing up, at which point we shut down the engines and start jigging. There often tends to be a whole lot of spikes (one-half to two pounders) during this time of the year and as you work through the numbers you will hit pockets of larger trout. I have had many days on end where getting 60 to 80 trout is the norm."

Light tackle techniques work best off of Lucy, and a one-quarter to one-ounce bucktail is mandatory in your quiver. Marks usually run thick here, and a fully lit up screen will tell you at what

When netting a fluke, the angler should guide the flattie headfirst into the net. Captain Al Crudele exhibits proper form while snatching this flatfish

depth the weakfish, croakers and bluefish are staging. Drop a bucktail jig in white, chartreuse or yellow with a two to four inch piece of squid or four-inch Fin-S fish plastic on the end and allow the bucktail to get worked in the current, jigging intermittently. You may have to experiment and find the water depth at which the majority of the schools hit. Most often, you'll get whacked on the way down, and feel a small, but awakening bump. Palm the line and start jigging there immediately. September through early November offer weakfish and croakers on the plate, as well as shots of false albacore. Smaller one to three pound blues ravage through from July to September and the choppers of eight to 20 pounds show up in October and November. Stripers will hug the coast during the fall migration southward and inhale larger two to four ounce bucktails dropped to the bottom.

Another productive method to take the weakies, croakers and even a few fluke is to drop a high-lo rig down, fixed with 2/0 to 3/0 baitholder hooks. Use bloodworms and squid or clam strips for bait, simply bouncing along the bottom with a 3-ounce bank sinker. Ideally you want to drift north to south, and can drift a fairly large section of this area, but once you see that Lucy is ahead of you at an almost 45-degree angle on either drift, motor back up and get ahead of her again to restart a drift.

HOT SHOT TIP

When bouncing bucktails for weakfish and croakers, add a dropper loop 2 feet up and affix a white 2/0 teaser to double your hook-up ratio.

30

Great Egg Reef

GPS: 39'14.50 / 74'21.50
LORAN: 26955 / 42950
Distance: 8 miles southeast from Absecon Inlet, 9.2 miles east/southeast from Great Egg Inlet
Depth: 45 to 72 feet
Target Species: Blackfish, Sea Bass, Fluke, Little Tunny, Skipjack Tuna, Bonito
Prime Time of Year: March/April (BLK), May through October (SEB, FLK), JULY through September (LIT, BON, SKP)

As more and more anglers are discovering the importance, viability, and accessibility of New Jersey's artificial reef sites, an impressive line of boats are making the trek to their local reef on day trips to bang out a varied catch. Recreational anglers are now making the same trip out to take advantage of these man-made piscatorial playgrounds. The Great Egg reef, which lies 7.2 miles off the shore of Atlantic City, is a fantastic one-mile square bottom-fishing haven brimming with structure. Most of the debris consists of is large clusters of army tanks on the west and south sides.

Plenty of tire piles, reef balls, and pipe section also hug the bottom. The largest asset is the wreck of a 165-foot tanker that is prominently placed as the centerpiece of the reef.

Most of the material is spread out, with the exception of the tank clusters, so you have to find your particular spot and set up on it to really concentrate on the opportunity inhabiting it. Many sharpies will target a certain tank and anchor right on it, and then proceed to pull in anywhere from 25 to 100 tog. Since most people drift fish this reef site, you can put yourself at an advantage by anchoring on the little pieces if you can pinpoint them and are proficient with setting the anchor. Tog find the tanks appealing during the early months of March and April when the water hits the upper 40s and low 50s.

HOT SHOT TIP

Start your morning by trolling the area for schoolie bluefin, tunny or bonito, then by mid-morning, begin to set up and drift for fluke or anchor up for blackfish.

Blackfish and sea bass are the main fare here, but a smorgasbord of species will pass through during the heat of the summer. Croakers invade the place from August through early October, and little tunny, skipjacks, and chick dolphin to six pounds will be taken on the troll. The doldrums of July, when the humidity and heat soaks you like a wet blanket, is the best time to hit the GE Reef for doormat fluke, which rest in the deeper sections where the cooler mid-60-degree water is. Many anglers are now discovering the potential to hang a doormatter on this particular reef site and you will see legions of drifters bouncing big four to six-ounce bucktails here in the summertime.

You can pull a variety of species off this particular reef. One late July day, I hit the reef in a friend's 24 Hydrasport in attempt to tackle a quality fluke. The NOAA predictions were a bit off from their two to three foot forecast, and as we were getting swamped in solid northeast four to sixes, I continued to bounce my bucktail. In two drops, I pulled up a four-foot brown shark and a five-pound mahi-mahi off the bottom. Talk about variety! Then we took a wave over the stern that put six inches of water in our boat from front to back. What if we stayed out there, what else might we have caught? Probably another six-footer that would've put us under, but maybe something else. The promise of the unknown will keep me going back.

31

Dog Lump

GPS: 74'20.50 / 39'11.50
LORAN: 26945 / 42920
Distance: 10 miles east/southeast from Great Egg or Absecon Inlet
Depth: 54 to 76 feet
Target Species: Little Tunny, Bluefin Tuna, Dolphin, Skipjack Tuna, Bluefish
Prime Time of Year: July through October (LIT, BFT, DPH, SKP, BLF)

Talk about a man's best friend. A certain special little spot (no pun intended) lies about 10 miles on a slight southeast course out of the Great Egg Inlet—The Dog Lump. On most nautical charts, the Dog Lump rises up off of the sea floor and in its outline resembles a running dog, with legs, ears, nose, tail, poop and all. No joke. But, more importantly, the curves, dips, and ledges of the outline of the Dog represent excellent fish-bearing habitat conducive to upwelling of currents that drive bait and nutrients to the surface.

The extremes of the Dog Lump drop to 76 feet along its north side, 74 feet along the southeast side and rises to a height of 54 feet at its pinnacle. The average depth runs between 58 to 61 feet on the whole lump. The relatively short surface area of the Dog allows you to cover the lump from the belly to the back of the Dog in roughly a half an hour going five to six knots, so you can pick sections of the lump to work in a zigzag pattern to cover the whole area in the course of an hour or two. The tiny lump of 60 feet that rests just east, under the "tail" of the Dog, resembles what dogs do best, and can very easily be reached and hit in a matter of minutes to stretch your coverage while making a turn.

Skipjack tuna hammer trolled feathers with a vengeance. Sean Reilly holds this speeding bullet up just before release.

So what's the Dog dishing out? Well, summertime is when the dog truly has a chance to show its talent, and anywhere from July to October, it becomes a drag-peeling piscatorial party. When the mid-summer warm water temps bounce between the high 60s and 70s, the Great Atlantic ushers in the high-octane smorgasbord of Jersey's speedster species that infiltrate and take over the inshore waters. Bonito, Spanish mackerel, false albacore, skipjack tuna and mahi-mahi are here to play ball. When the water temps hover in the 70s and the warm water eddies bring in the bluewater, mahi will rear their pugnacious faces with consistency, and are generally chicken to gaffer size of two to 15 pounds. And here's something else to boil your blood. Not only is the Dog Lump a speedster hangout, but it is also a cruising ground for bluefin tuna. Generally the bluefin are in the football size but can range up to 60 pounds if you hit it right.

HOT SHOT TIP

When trolling feathers or cedar plugs, make slow, 45-degree turns frequently as schoolie bluefin, dolphin, and skipjacks will strike when the lure slows down with the slack in the line.

Whatever you're targeting, the tactic that takes the title here is trolling. Three to five inch small feathers, Size 0 or 00 Clark spoons, and four-inch squid pink or purple skirts on spreader bars or trolled alone do the most damage to fool the speedsters. Some excellent approaches that have worked for Sean Reilly of the *Kirra* include starting on the south side and heading northwest to hit the most drastic edges. Though you're scoping after fastfare, invariably you will find the bluefish, and though they are not lame slackers by any means, they can be a costly nuisance when trolling your expensive feathers and squid skirts.

One fine summer day in 2004 I fished on Reilly's *Kirra* in search of bluefin that were coursing through the area, but got nothing but bluefish on most of our patterns. Skunked. So what'd we do? We set course for the tail end of the Dog and had not a hit. "What'd you want to do?" Reilly asked. Pointing at the tiny lump that looked like the poop, I said, "This looks attractive." We stretched our troll to the Dog Poop lump to make our turn, and a 30-pound bluefin tuna slammed into our lure dead on. The moral? Always clean up after your Dog.

32

Tabletop

GPS: 39'09.20 / 74'30.72
LORAN: 27001 / 42890
Distance: 7 miles southeast of the Great Egg Inlet, 9 miles east of Townsend's Inlet
Depth: 36 to 68 feet
Target Species: Fluke, Little Tunny, Bluefish, Spanish Mackerel
Prime Time of Year: May through September (FLK), July through September (LIT, BLF, SPN)

This flattened gem consistently puts fish on the dinner table, and ironically enough, the place is called the Tabletop. It's a skinny two-mile oblong hump that runs southwest to northeast, which is set smack dab on top of a notch in the 10-fathom line. The level surface of it's top hits 36 feet, but surrounding it on all sides is water depth from 50 to 68 feet, and some spots drop to a 70-foot level or more. The whole tabletop resembles a giant flatiron with gullies on all sides, and it spells great hiding and ambushing structure for many species. South Jersey beaches are notorious for their gradual, shallow beach slope out from the shoreline, which doesn't bode too well for holding bait and gamefish, and that is why the Tabletop happens to be a hangout. Once fish migrate out to the area, they can now rest on the sharply dropping edges and ambush their prey. Which brings me to the point of what the Tabletop is famous for—large fluke.

Ed Bronstein of Fin-Atics knows of the fluke attraction to the spot. "On the pinnacle, your depthfinder will read a skinny 36 feet. Flatfish will, for the most part, lie on all sides, mostly north, west and east where it will continually drop off into the 50s then decline into 60 and 70 foot depths. Fluke fishermen bring live snapper bluefish out there, from about three to four inches long, and drop 'em down while drifting over the edges. Some big fluke get taken there. During late summer, it's the place fluke stop at on their migration outward, because of all the great depressions around." You can easily hit both east and west ledges on a drift, and if that particular drift doesn't produce, motor up a little further down and try it again, covering a different edge. There's plenty of room to work all angles on the table. May through September is the hottest season for the flatfish, and you can bet on bagging larger specimens on the spring and fall migrations.

HOT SHOT TIP
Hook a live snapper bluefish through the lips and drift him on a fishfinder rig, starting on the top and gradually over the northwest or east drops for a doormat fluke.

Tons of bait settles in the area and at any given time you can have peanut bunker, sand eels, rainfish or spearing oiling up the waters. Come September and October, the Tabletop becomes an inshore troller's haven. Trollers cruise around the edges and ledges on all sides dragging feathers, Clark spoons, and Got-chas's tying into the southern speedsters of little tunny, bonito, and Spanish mackerel. In recent years, small chicken dolphin have even been taken off the table. If you are looking on stocking up on bait in the early season, mackerel come cruising through during March and April and you can put a barrel full of mackerel baits on board to use for the fluke and shark season.

A good piece of advice is to sniff around the outskirts of the Tabletop, as there are a few older wrecks on east side and south side, most notably a Car Wreck Float, which was a barge carrying a load of vintage era cars that sank decades ago. There's not much left of the debris from the decaying effects of the sea, but there is still enough there to hold the doormat of your dreams.

33

Sea Isle Lump

GPS: 39'07.39 / 74'38.13
LORAN: 27042 / 42868
Distance: 2.5 miles east from Townsend's Inlet
Depth: 18 to 51 feet
Target Species: Striped Bass, Weakfish, Fluke
Prime Time of Year: Late April and May, September October (WEK), July through October (FLK), October through December (STB)

The number one spot that should be on any shrewd boat fisherman's hit list coming out of Townsend's Inlet is the Sea Isle Lump, namely because it is so accessible and prolific. It can be reached just less than three miles out, bearing 80 degrees from the Townsend's Inlet A Buoy. The Lump is a 1.75-mile long oblong-shaped mound in the Atlantic that ranges in depth from 58 feet around its edges to 18 feet at its most shallow. Most of the bottom structure consists of encrusted mussel beds and hard sand.

It's a very precarious situation here for the striped bass angler, in that the "nun" buoy that marks the Sea Isle Lump is almost dead-on the 3 mile Federal boundary, which means, if you are targeting stripers, you had better stay on the west side of the nun buoy to play it safe. The southwest corner of the Lump where the depth rises from 46 feet to 18 feet is a hot spot to target striped bass, and is where you can legally go after bass within the three mile Federal line. In the fall, jig three to six ounce Kroc-o-dile spoons or wide-profile Crippled Herrings here, as the fall peanut bunker, sand eel and mullet runs will be the main fare for the feeding stripers and the metals jigs will mimic them perfectly.

Fluke can be found there in the summertime hanging on the eastern and northwestern edges. A wise bit of advice is to head just a hair southeast for about a half mile, where a set of three other small 27-foot mounds dot the area. This allows you to set up on longer drifts and will benefit you in covering more fluctuation in water depth, from shallow to deep to shallow over and over again. You'll find plenty more fluke there, and the crowds won't be nearly as heavy. During late summer, weakfish, as well as croakers, can be found keeping cool in the deeper waters surrounding the Lump that reach depths between 45 to 51 feet. Drop a few pieces of sandworms on floating jighead rigs to get their attention.

It gets better too. What could be better than throwing in some off-kilter species in the mix? For three weeks in July and early August of 2004, a solid school of cobia hung tight around the nun buoy, and they weren't small. Cobia to 65 pounds were hammering live eels thrown at them. The water temps were in the 70 to 75 degree range and the cobia set up by the buoy snacking down on all the life that concentrates around the buoy's perimeter. Keep an eye out for those men in the brown suits, stalking your bait like standstill sharks.

HOT SHOT TIP

During the fall run jigging for stripers, paint your Kroc-O-Dile wide profile spoons completely white. The color works wonders on bass.

34

Avalon Shoal

GPS: 39'05.54 / 74'34.21
LORAN: 27012 / 42848
Distance: 5.5 miles east of Townsend's Inlet
Depth: 26 to 54 feet
Target Species: Bluefish, Weakfish, Bonito, Little Tunny, Spanish Mackerel, Triggerfish, Fluke
Prime Time of Year: Late April, May (WEK), May through October (BLF, FLK), July through September (BON, LIT, SPN, TRG)

Resting 5.5 miles off the coast of Avalon, is a series of mounds and rises that are strewn about a three-quarter square mile area, resting just inside the 10-fathom line known as the Avalon Shoal. Coming out of Townsend's Inlet on a 119-degree bearing, the shoal is just over a 5-mile ride. A sure sign you're around it is to notice the red 2 Buoy, which flashes every 6 seconds and marks the edge of the shipping lane east of which hits 56 feet. Just a few hairs west inside of the buoy, a plateau of 26 feet sits as a pedestal to which various species flock.

Eric Kuenhart of Red Dog Bait and Tackle considers this a potpourri type of place, where all makes and models of inshore dwellers from bottom to top reside. "Any day during the summer, from July through September, you'll see a parking lot full of boaters there, but it doesn't seem to push the fish down. Bluefish are all over the place at this time, and I mean everywhere. You have to keep an eye out for bird play, as the blues will spring up and down in an instant, but most of the time they'll push the baitfish up to the surface and keep them there. Little tunny, bonito, and Spanish macks are all mixed in with the blues, and it's worth it to drag some small feathers or Ava Jigs behind the boat outside of the blitzing blues."

But before the summer season gets underway, the Avalon Shoal is known to spring anglers as a top-notch weakfish haunt, as they migrate on their spring run by the thousands inshore to enter the backwaters. Mostly you'll run into weak-fish of spike size (one-half to one pound) to tide runners that will push the scale at over 10 pounds. Late April and early May will put you into these weakies, and a well placed bucktail with a plastic 4-inch Fin-S fish in Rainbow Trout or Bubble Gum colors on the back will tease them into a strike.

HOT SHOT TIP

Late summer, try a first troll around the 2 Buoy in circles to pick up wandering chick mahi-mahi (2 to 4 pound) that cluster around the cover of the buoy.

Come late summer, fluke spill out of the back bays and begin their move outward, and always seem to set up for a few weeks on the shoal. When the air begins to get a tiny bit colder, you know its time to drift the channel edges on the outside of the 2 Buoy for some serious sized doormats. Kuenhart also recommends fishing around the 2 buoy itself for a steady pull of trig-gerfish that meander about the rope in the shadow of the buoy.

For some added excitement, Kuenhart adds, "Once in a while heading in from an offshore trip in summertime, I'll see small 40 to 60 pound mako sharks jump and twist out of the water at Avalon Shoal. People don't realize they come that close in, but they do. There's also a showing of brown sharks and sand tiger sharks during the late spring months." There's some food for thought.

35

Sea Isle Ridge

GPS: 38'59.30 / 74'26.00
LORAN: 26950 / 42778
Distance: 15 miles southeast from Great Egg Bell Buoy
Depth: 45 to 80 feet
Target Species: Small Bluefin Tuna, Little Tunny, Spanish Mackerel, Bonito, Skipjack Tuna, Dolphin
Prime Time of Year: August through Oct (ALL)

Τhis place is speedster heaven. The amoeba-shaped Sea Isle Ridge's center lies approximately 12.5 miles off the coast of Sea Isle in a northwest to southeast fashion, offering attainable access and fruitful framework for the day troller's agenda. Depth ranges from 45 to 80 feet within its ridges and off along the outside of its perimeter. The eastern edge of the ridge is where it comes up to its shallowest at 54 feet. The Southwest corner has a phenomenal little notch where the waters dip from 54 to 65 feet in a groove, and due to the design of the contour, nutrients and baitfish hold steady there caused by the dramatic upwelling. There's a funky little group of fingers that lie on the northeast corner that allow you to pull your spread over a bunch of hills at once, eliminating the hassle of changing course after every pass.

September is the month set aside for the rocket-propelled rascals more commonly known as bonito, Spanish mackerel, false albacore, and skipjack tuna.

Your standard brands of baitfish that stack up at the Ridge are peanut bunker, spearing, rainfish, bay anchovies, and other assorted baitfish, thus smaller lures work better out here. The speedsters love anything with a bright flash and fast retrieval speed. You need everything in the bucket to mimic the tinier baitfish around, and small feathers will fit the bill when trolling. Two to three inch feathers in red/white, blue/white or any with Mylar flash tied in work nicely. Troll feathers or small metals at a rapid pace around six to seven knots so they streak through the water in a teasing fashion, periodically hopping out of the water and surfing along your wake.

Spreader bars rigged with small squid skirts or feathers will attract loads of schoolie bluefin tuna to the boat. This football bluefin was the 23rd caught in one day on the Carcharodon.

Little tunny and skipjack tuna

will probably be the first torpedoes to hit your spread. If you happen upon a school of them, angle your boat a hundred yards in front of the school, and troll in front of the school so you won't scare the school down. For added excitement, grab a lightweight rod and start casting small metals, reeling in as fast as possible. You'll lose your marbles when a tunny or skippie hamhocks your line. The school moves faster than you can keep up, so you'll be bumping that motor in and out of gear every minute or two to speed up and cut them off.

Bonito can be easily identified by their series of black wavy lines from mid-body to the tailfin area, whereas skipjacks have the wavy lines on the bottom part of their body, and tunny have the wavy lines on the upper body, but also exhibit four or five black spots by their pectoral fin. When you find a school of bonito, be sure to bring a medium weight rod spooled with 14-pound test line and a 12-pound fluorocarbon leader with a size 1/0 tuna hook tied on the end. Hook on a single spearing and hold on tight.

HOT SHOT TIP

If you are into bluefin tuna or dolphin on the troll, stop the boat, dice up fresh peanut bunkers cut in quarters, chuck 'em over board, followed by a live peanut with a pinch-on weight or freelined with a 3/0 Octopus hook through the lips. Hang on tight!

Spanish mackerel are vibrantly colored fish with yellows, blues, and oranges throughout their makeup, and usually run between two and six pounds on the Ridge. Chicken and gaffer size dolphin of two to 15 pounds will hit the troll, and will also respond to accurately placed bucktails once the school presents itself. If you hook into a dolphin on the troll, keep it on the line and cast out bucktails around him. Other dolphin will usually follow the hooked one to boatside.

There's just so much to do at the Sea Isle Ridge. Not only is it a prolific fish-bearing piece of real estate, it's also a short run that most small-boat anglers can get out to if the conditions favor you. And I forgot to mention, the Ridge is known for producing the Atlantic speedsters, but white marlin have been fought and subdued in its waters. How's that for a 12.5-mile ride out?

36

Varanger— a.k.a. the 28 Mile Wreck

GPS: 39'00.45 / 74'04.97
LORAN: 26825 / 42803
Distance: 28 miles from Absecon, Great Egg, Inlets
Depth: 95 to 130 feet
Target Species: Mako, Thresher, Dusky Sharks, Bluefish, Blackfish, Cod
Prime Time of Year: June, July (SHK), June through October (BLF),
    November through February (BLK, COD)

Here's a tip—if you're around
Atlantic City and are planning to do some gambling, there's one
number that always hits hard. Twenty-eight. Why? Because every
time you venture out approximately 28 miles off Atlantic City
from Absecon, Great Egg or Corson's Inlet, you'll inevitably find
the wreck of the *Varanger*. It's a win-win situation. The *Varanger*,
commonly known as the 28 Mile Wreck, was a 470 foot
Norwegian tanker sunk by German U-boat 130 in World War
II, and the good news is that the entire crew of 40 escaped alive.
Now, the vessel sits upright in 120 feet of water but rises to 95
feet and the surrounding water dips into the 135-plus mark.

The 28 Mile Wreck draws sharks in from their migratory push in late spring and early fall, and is known as one of the most prominent sharking spots for the south Jersey fleet. Schoolie bluefin tuna regularly cruise by the perimeter of the wreck in the fall months and chunk baits will bring them on board. On the wreck itself, yellowfin tuna will hit the troll with smaller feathers in green and yellow, and July thru September can haul in dolphin from chicken-size to whopping bulls of 40 pounds.

Heading into the late fall and winter months, the *Varanger* changes its inhabitants and becomes an outstanding offshore blackfish and sea bass hot spot, where tog to 24 pounds have been pulled up from in recent years. Large cod can also be angled here when the temps begin to plummet into the high 50s.

The *Varanger* is a successfully productive site by itself, but you have to keep your eyes open around the area. Eric Kuenhart of Red Dog Bait and Tackle points out, "There's a lot of structure around the wreck, just northeast of it a quarter mile off is another small wreck, and in the south, there are mounds that come up 96 feet. That's not all, the Cigar is just a short run south of it, and the 20-fathom line lies just east. If I could give any advice, it'd be don't just fish the wreck. The *Varanger* draws fish to the area, but the changing structure holds them there with upwelling all around the 20 fathom edges."

Spring makos are a main attraction, through dusky, brown, threshers and occasional hammerheads will also show up. And there are some other unusual visitors around during the summer months, as the New Jersey state record wahoo of 123 pounds 12 ounces was caught here by Robert Carr in 1992.

HOT SHOT TIP

Come November, make the trek out 28 miles to drop whole green or Dungeness crabs for tautog. There is surely a world record waiting on this far-reaching wreck.

37

Cigar

GPS: Top of lump, 38'54.20 / 74'08.00; North Tip, 38'57.00 / 74'04.30; Southern Tip, 38'51.40 / 74'12.00
LORAN: 26835 / 43745
Distance: 35 miles east from Cape May Inlet, 29 miles east from Townsend's Inlet
Depth: 94 to 100 on top of lump; 120 to 140 surrounding lump
Target Species: Sharks
Prime Time of Year: Late May through early July, Late August through October (SHK)

What a smokin' spot! The Cigar has the distinction of being a devilishly top-rate sharking location that literally smokes anglers' lines off their reels. It's a very long lump, stretching 7 miles, and runs in depth from 94 to 130 feet. The lump itself is a stogie-shaped island of the 20-fathom line that seems to have broken off from the rest of the 20-fathom pack.

This place holds some great stories concerning fish with big teeth. In 2003, I hit this area with Captain Al Crudele of the *Bayhound* on his 21-foot skiff with calm seas. On the radio was nervous chatter concerning eyewitness accounts of a very large shadow patrolling the Cigar area waters. And during the day captains from tuna towers reported a dark shape of over 18 feet long cruising through their slicks. Great White sharks are known to migrate up through this area in June. It was June. That's all I'm saying. We did manage to battle over a dozen blue sharks that day, but there was definitely an uneasiness in the air when the hunters imagined that they could become the hunted.

HOT SHOT TIP

For threshers, from the running line crimp on a 500-pound class Sampo, then a 12 foot shot of 280-pound cable, another 500-pound Sampo crimped on, then a four foot shot of 240-pound wire, to which a double hook Mustad 10/0 offset is haywired on. The bait is a whole 8 to 10 pound class bluefish fillet.

Sharks find this area appealing, not only for the sudden, 7-mile rise off the bottom, but the wreck of the *Champion* sits on the southwest corner of the Cigar, providing more structure. Although known for makos, blue sharks, and the occasional great white spotting, the Cigar really shines as a thresher shark spot. Threshers are generally accepted as being inshore species of shark, and the relatively close distance to the mainland keeps them tight on the Cigar. Want proof? The New Jersey state record thresher was caught here in 2004 by Chris Chalmers, and it weighed 617 pounds, breaking the previous record of 614 pounds, which interestingly enough was caught only a few miles away at the 28 Mile Wreck.

Starting on the northeast corner in 130 feet of water, the best drifts will take you over the middle of the top of the Cigar to where it rises to 90 to 100 feet, then as you drift off the southwest edge, you drop into 140 feet of water and hopefully cross over the wreck of the *Champion* on your way. Depending on the wind and current, the opposite drift going southwest to northeast will work just as well. Thresher sharks seem to patrol at shallower depths, and thus the flatlines you send out may give you an added advantage for targeting the whiptails. They favor the chillier water climes of high 50s to low 60s, so early season bets in late May and early June or into late September early October will allow you your best chances on the Cigar.

Regardless of what you tie into at the Cigar, you can rest assured it's going to bring you the fight of your life, and will probably merit breaking out the Cohibas to light up for the ride home.

38

5 Fathom Bank

GPS: 38'54.50 / 74'38.60
LORAN: 27010 / 42715
Distance: 11 miles northeast of Cape May Inlet, 5 miles east
   of Corson's Inlet
Depth: 18 to 66 feet
Target Species: Bluefish, Little Tunny, Bonita, Skipjack Tuna, Fluke,
   Brown and Dusky Shark
Prime Time of Year: May through November (BLF), July through
   September (LIT, BON, SKP) May, September (FLK), August (SHK)

I f you're looking for an all-around knockout spot, the Five Fathom Bank will be it. It's a vast area, covering a stretch of roughly four to five miles, and its varied depth blankets an area where you can easily run from 20 feet to 60 feet of water to hunt for different species.

The immense territory consists of widespread shoals and holes, humps and bumps. Throw in some quick drop-offs, and you've got a playing field that holds an abundant mix of fish year round. The 4FB Buoy, on the southernmost side of the bank, is anchored just outside the last shoal and boasts some excellent shelves to drop where the depth slips from 30 feet to 80 feet in a blink of an eye. The 2FB marks the particular shoal from where the waters on the east side of it drop to 66 feet and rise up to 33 feet on the bank.

The overall expanse residing on the west side of the dropoffs average 18 to 30 feet and spread out an inviting series of hills and lumps, which attract baitfish, and thus just about every other predatory inshore species. Bluefish are the righteous locals that regularly patrol the grounds. And usually, they ain't the small ones either. Blues from chopper size of 5 to 6 pounds to alligator proportions of 18 to 20 pounds terrorize the area. If you need proof, just know that the New Jersey state record bluefish was muscled out of here, a gorilla caught by Roger Kastorsky in 1997 and weighing in at 27 pounds, 1 ounce. What a monster!

Bluefish become downright evil when they get this big. This 18 pound alligator bluefish hit a whole bluefish fillet intended for a mako, and was fought by John Pochinski, Jr. on the Sandpiper.

Don't waste any type of plastic shads or soft-bodied lures here, as bluefish invade the Bank's waters from May through November, and you will lose much of your arsenal. Stick to metals and hard-composite lures. Troll Ava 27 to 67 jigs, Ponytails, or Clark Spoons around the area to minimize lure loss. If you feel like tackling the blues in a different manner, you can also set up on a chunk slick for the bluefish, dropping down bunker chunks on steel-leadered 5/0 hooks. Try to anchor along the eastern edge where the drop begins. The low-down on the spot has it that brown sharks and dusky sharks will also inhale the chunk baits here, so chance may have it that you may get knee-deep into one heck of a fight you didn't expect.

HOT SHOT TIP
Drop a chum bucket over the side to start a bunker chum slick, set up with fresh bunker backs and sink down chunks with 2 to 6 ounce weights for bluefish, with a chunk or two on the bottom for brown and dusky sharks.

Come late summer, doormat fluke lay along the shoals, and big strip baits and bucktails bring in some serious sized flatties on the high ground. Break out the Clark spoons and troll along the eastern ridges from late July to October to stir up little tunny, bonito, skippies and some chick dolphin with consistency. Even though they'd work magic, I'd avoid throwing out spreader bars here, unless you can afford to lose some.

Though not legal by Federal standards, a mad dog striper bite occurs here in the fall when the fish are migrating and if the EEZ zone ever opens up for stripers, the Five Fathom Bank would be the place to be. But for now, concentrate on that bluefish.

39

East Lump

GPS: 38 47.35 / 74 27.55
LORAN: 26940 / 42655
Distance: 20 miles southeast from Cape May Inlet, 22 miles southeast
from Townsend's Inlet
Depth: 60 feet on top of hill; 80 to 100 feet around lump
Target Species: Shark, Bluefish, Bluefin Tuna
Prime Time of Year: Mid-May through October (BLF), June, July (SHK),
July through September (BFT)

A nice, accommodating location to tackle some larger toothy types of species goes by the name of the East Lump and lays 23 miles outside of the Cape May Inlet. Resting on the 15-fathom line and barely west of a little 20-fathom island, the East Lump's dimensions extend a mile or so in length and stretch approximately 400 yards wide. The highest point of the hump is about 56 feet on its ridge, and it dips down to 105 feet just off its southeast side.

George Algard of Sterling Harbor Bait and Tackle says, "From mid-spring through late fall, bluefish of all sizes infiltrate and take residence at the lump. Most anglers troll during the daytime with Ponytails in yellow/green or black/orange color combos, and will also chunk at night for the blues. In the heat of the summer, it is better to troll your lures down further into the cooler water where the bluefish relocate to cool down."

Five to 15-pound bluefish are a mainstay at the Lump, but the distance offshore combined with the oily slick and smell of the blues bring in more formidable characters. Algard mentions, "Because of the immense amount of blues that reside there, the East Lump becomes a fairly productive inshore shark fishing ground with makos, duskies, and occasional hammerhead and tiger sharks mixed in, taking chunk baits and bluefish fillets. June is the desired month to have at the shark fishery there, but it will run into early July as well. If you're heading to the East Lump, be prepared to bring the bluefish and shark tackle."

HOT SHOT TIP

Troll with cedar plugs in the wash at around 6 knots on the flatlines to have them hopping in and out of the water. Schoolie bluefin tuna will hammer them in the propwash.

Come August into early fall the East Lump is a schoolie bluefin tuna stomping ground, as they join in with their older 40 to 70-pound brothers who regularly inhabit the area. Fishermen who pull cedar plugs and hexheads will tie into a solid pull of bluefin who stay around the lump gobbling down the bait that congregates there. Here's a trick from Algard— when you hook up with one, bump the motors out of gear for a second or two to allow the cedar plug or hexhead to sink a few feet, then jump it back into gear. Most bluefin can't resist the opportunity to attack a stunned bait. As well, bonito and little tunny start hitting size 00 Clark spoons on the troll, if you aren't having much luck on the bluefin and want to scale down a bit and use light tackle.

And to give you some extra incentive, know that every now and then, some white marlin are hooked here under the right conditions of warm temperature breaks and blue water in the mid 70 degree range. If you see a bill breaking water, quickly drop a rigged ballyhoo back in the pattern to see what you can come up with.

40

Cape May Reef

GPS: 38'53.75 / 74'39.98
LORAN: 27026 / 42696
Distance: 9 miles southeast of Cape May Inlet
Depth: 48 to 76 feet
Target Species: Blackfish, Sea Bass and Triggerfish
Prime Time of Year: November through January (BLK), May through
   October (SEB, TRG)

Bucktoothed brawlers call it paradise. (That's blackfish to you.) Yet another reef site exists for south Jersey bottom fishing anglers. Laying in a three-mile square area, nine miles southeast of the Cape May Inlet, is the jagged playground called the Cape May Reef. The Cape May Reef is a man-made serrated structure consisting of 17 wrecks including the 106-foot clam dredge *Laita*, 157-foot buoy tender *Red Oak*, the 165-foot barge *Rothenbach*, and is highlighted by the 205-foot tanker *Onandaga*. The 17 wrecks are split up almost evenly with 10 on the north side and 7 on the south side. The rubble from the Ben Franklin Bridge is spilled about the north side and in between exist approximately 3,500 tire units, and tons of reef balls, tanks and subway cars, all of which make up a mind-boggling amount of structure. The plot itself is broken up all over a northeast to southwest pattern where the bulk of the sunken wrecks lay at the tips of the site. You'll be plying waters that range from 48 feet on the northwest end to 76 feet on the southeast side.

The name of the game here is blackfish and sea bass. Captain Sam Resicgno of the *Mary M III* pounds the Cape May Reef with a highly targeted strategy. The bridge rubble sections offer unlimited lairs for blackies to hide. It's very sticky in the riff-raff, with plenty of gaping holes for your sinker to fall into. You will be losing rigs. Rescigno usually likes to hit the concrete rubble first–with a purpose. The north end is shallower for warmer waters, and in winter months, Sam will target this area first where water is warmer. A smart approach is to bounce just of the edges of structure on the downtide side of the bridge rubble, tankers and ledges as a strong Cape May current wafts food over the scrap where the blackfish wait eagerly to pick the forage off the bottom and suck in all the goodies. November through January show the finest blackfishing. May through October hold black sea bass before they migrate.

You're going to lose a lot of rigs on the sticky jagged structure, so try to keep the rigs as simple as possible. Use a braided line of 50-pound test, and Albright a 25-foot section of 30-pound mono. Double up a three-foot section and tie off at the top with a double overhand knot. Loop on a bank sinker off the bottom. Three inches up from the bank sinker, pinch the line into a loop and loop on a snelled #6 Virginia hook. You're in business. This rig allows a breakaway approach, to simply loop on another sinker when it gets busted off. You'll go nuts breaking and retying sinkers, but you'll eliminate the insanity of constantly tying on completely new rigs. When a sinker busts off, simply retie the broken section off with a double overhand knot and put on another sinker. Simple enough.

This place is awesome. Tautog heaven. Feel your way through the ledges, and drop two anchors if you can to pinpoint a spot on the reef.

For sea bass, tie a Hi/Lo rig of 30-pound test, size 1/0 hooks, and tie a simple overhand loop for your bank sinker weight. Bounce around with clam chunks, squid strips or even spearing. You can doctor up your rig with all the fancy skirts, and spinners if you desire as well, but these types of rigs will usually work best when there is a drift to propel the skirts and spinners into action. A very interesting point to note is that during the months of July and August, spadefish and king mackerel can be found on and over this reef site.

HOT SHOT TIP
Start your day by working the Bridge Rubble section on the northern part of the reef site. Quantity blackfish hold there as there are more nooks and crannies for them to hide in.

41

Old Grounds

GPS: 38'34.40 / 74'47.72
LORAN: 27025 / 42496
Distance: 18 miles south of Cape May Inlet
Depth: 63 to 100 feet
Target Species: Fluke, Sea Bass
Prime Time of Year: May through October (FLK), May through November (SEB)

Positioned smack dab within the inbound and outbound shipping lanes of Delaware Bay is the fabled Old Grounds. In the olden days, to enter the shallower water of Delaware Bay, old-time sailing ships coming from overseas would need to lighten their loads to safely enter and navigate the inlet of the bay's skinnier waters. In order to effectively do that, the ships would drop their rock ballasts before coming to shore, and thus, after vessel upon vessel unloaded their ballasts of rock blocks for years, the Old Grounds were born. At least, so the story goes.

Whatever the case, it's no fable that a fantastic mixture of structure consisting of rock bottom and mussel beds comprise the area of this archaic artificial reef, and that the Old Grounds are one of the state's finest fluke and sea bass grounds. Though quantities of fluke and sea bass are apparent, the true allure of the spot is that you've got a very credible shot at the elusive doormat-size fluke.

Trophy flounder are the main target here. The tackle shops in Cape May consistently report patrons steaming back to dock with load catches of fluke from the Old Grounds. I know from talking with Jim Wallace regularly at Jim's Bait and Tackle in Cape May that his patrons limit out virtually every time they hit the area, and bags average in the three to five pound class.

When hitting the area, a first telltale sign that you are creeping up to the spot is the noticeable presence of the Delaware party boat packet, as the OG is a short run for them. Another true mark is the yellow Delaware Bay (DB) buoy where the fleet tends to congregate. The area around the buoy will range from 65 to 75 feet, but north and a

Doormat fluke are no joke at the Old Grounds, and 8 to 12 pound flatties happen more often than you think, as Kristie Andresen showed the author how it's done.

tiny bit east of the area, the depth will sound to 90-plus feet. Use braided line to up the odds in your favor, as the increased sensitivity and ability to cut through water will aid you in the deep-water conditions. And bring a healthy bunch of bank sinkers from four to 16 ounces, as it can get sticky with the rocky structure.

HOT SHOT TIP
Instead of using a bank sinker for weight, connect a four to eight ounce chrome ball jig rigged with a bait strip for added attraction to a doormat.

May through October is the season for fluke and sea bass, though sea bass can also be caught through November as well. The key to flattie success here is to think big. It pays off to throw down large strips of squid, herring, sea robin, or dogfish for the barn door of your dreams. Medium size flatties of three to seven pounds, which are regularly taken, will hang themselves on the strip, so it's a win-win situation for you to target big fish. It'll also keep the smaller throwbacks off the hook.

Drift over the ballast piles and mussel beds, and when you hit a pod be sure to mark the spot, as the fluke will gather in packs. For the most part you will find the sea bass over the rockpiles and the fluke on the edges. Make sure you are effectively dropping down around the rocks, and not on them, if you are searching for fluke. Whether you are meat fishing for a cooler full of sea bass and fluke or hunting a doormatter, you've got your bases covered here.

42

Lobster Claw

GPS: 38'50.00 / 73'35.00
LORAN: 26640 / 42700
Distance: 47 miles southeast from Great Egg Inlet
Depth: 156 to 180 feet
Target Species: Yellowfin and Bluefin Tuna
Prime Time of Year: July through October (YFT, BFT)

Most anglers head a straight course to the canyons when they hear word of tuna. It's expected. But savvy anglers are on the tip that there are closer spots for tuna on the way out that rest nicely inshore of the Spencer and Lindenkohl Canyons, specifically a location named for its odd-shaped contour: the Lobster Claw. The unusual shape of the claw is actually the outline of the 30-fathom line, with the appearance of a lobster claw grabbing downward. The surrounding waters of the actual claw run from 26 to 29 fathoms, and on the northwest region, the water rises to 24 fathoms.

Don Brown of Gifford Marine is a seasoned veteran of the Lobster Claw, and has taken many an early and mid-season tuna from the grips of the claw. "During July and August, the Lobster Claw is a productive area for bluefin and yellowfin. One of the best spots to drag across is the area where the big pincher and small pincher meet in the notch. It's a nice edge, and it's a fairly tight area that you can run over a few times without wasting time."

Why does the Claw produce? Brown says, " The Claw sits on the outer edge of the bluefin migratory path. It basically mirrors along the 30 Fathom Line, and it becomes a super-highway for the bluefin, when they move through in the summertime. The Claw is really best described as an area with two big cuts into the 30 fathom line."

HOT SHOT TIP
Work a classic Pete Barrett "W" pattern for your trolling spread, setting out two cedar plugs or ballyhoo on the two bottom points and pulling a spreader bar, daisy chain, and spreader bar for the top three points.

Trolling feathers, tuna clones, spoons, Daisy Chains and the like over the edges during the morning usually snatches up a few bluefin and yellowfin, and the day chunk bite is hotter than the nighttime chunk. To give you an added advantage, Brown states, "Look for the secret smaller bumps off the beaten track around the Claw, up near the northwest side, and anchor up to start a chunk slick. The chunk works well on anchor, but I've had bluefin to 150 pounds even on the drift, while chunking and running over the edges."

Adds Brown, "Yellowfin seem to like the deeper drops off the edges, so if that's what we're targeting, we will forgo the sides of the edges, and troll the deeper water surrounding them." Besides the 30-fathom ledges, another reason the Claw becomes hot is from the commercial fishing pressure in the summer months. Scallop boats usually drag the area and that in turn churns up the water with scallops floating all over the place, producing a nice chum slick for the tuna.

Mostly, 30 to 70-pound class bluefin will be the common fare, though depending on water temps and prevailing currents, medium and large bluefin of 80 to 200 pounds can move through. You can find 40 to 60-pound yellowfin from July through November, as they will hold longer here than in northern Jersey waters, due to the southern water staying warmer further into the year. The 50 to 60-mile ride from Atlantic City, Great Egg and Cape May Inlets makes the Lobster Claw an accessible mid-range spot to mix it up with bluefin and yellowfin tuna without running the extra 20 to 30 miles to the Canyon edges.

43

Elephant's Trunk

GPS: Tip, 38'33.00 / 74'04.70
LORAN: 26780 / 42512
Distance: Southeast from Cape May Inlet, 41 miles to tip; 44 miles to west wall; 46 miles to east wall
Depth: 162 to 200 feet
Target Species: Mako, Thresher Sharks, Bluefin Tuna, Yellowfin Tuna, White Marlin
Prime Time of Year: June through August (SHK), July through October (BFT, YFT) July through September (WHM)

You could hear the trumpeting call beckon you as if you were stalking in the bush on Africa's vast savannahs, except for the fact that you are 40 some miles into the Atlantic Ocean. But nonetheless, there are elephants in the midst. A spot as big as it's namesake—The Elephant's Trunk— stretches southeast on a jaunt from 41 to 47 miles out of the south Jersey inlets off the peninsula of Cape May. Checking your local charts, you can see that the spot actually resembles an elephant's trunk with the mouth extended open as if it's going to grab a clump of peanuts out of your hand.

Liquid-quick white marlin are a prized catch out on the offshore grounds and this one put up one heck of a battle before Bernie Walker and his crew released it back into the waters of the Elephant Trunk.

The whole area of the Trunk runs north to south and its outline is actually drawn out by the 30 Fathom line. The prominent spot resembling the trunk juts out in an area that is a depression, which drops to 180 to 194 feet, surrounded by water between 150 and 180 feet on the east and west sides. By definition, it's an underwater valley. The impression formed by the trunk combined with current activity creates a stirring of the waters where phytoplankton, copepods, baitfish and, thus, sportfish congregate.

Anglers have an array of opportunities to fish the Trunk, as the east, west and tip and entire length of the trunk span a fair share of distance. Shark fishing is pursued with a passion here, as makos, threshers and blue sharks abound on the ledges of the east and west walls, which are not steep drops like at the canyons but decline in more of a slope that changes in depth in average from six to 30 feet from the main portion. Northwest to southeast drifts starting from the west side of the tip will allow you to cover the most productive ground, hitting ledges from 150 to 180, then dipping to 190 and back into 160-foot water. The Trunk isn't usually a heavily pressured spot for sharking, making it a prime place to set up on tournament day.

Probably one of the most attractive qualities of the Trunk is that come July it holds bluefin and yellowfin tuna. Why bother streaming the extra 40 miles to the nearest canyon, when you can be tackling tuna on the inside? Seamounts rise up to 162 feet in the vicinity on the west side of the tip, where the tuna tend to hang the most. Commercial scallop boats have been working this area year after year, and have led the bluefin tuna like some Pied Piper to the spot. If you can see bluefin breaking water behind the scallopers, then the chunk bite will be smokin'. If you've got the tuna corralled and packed into a spot, then set up on the chunk. Otherwise, since the size of the Trunk is so vast, trolling will allow you to cover more ground to raise a few tuna. Work a zigzag pattern starting from the northwest side of the Tip and head southward in and out of the 30-fathom line to find the tuna.

And not to be overlooked, when trolling ballyhoo or squids, keep an eye out for white marlin as they mill about the area during the summertime months leading into early fall.

HOT SHOT TIP

If commercial scallop boats are in the area, see if you can raise them on the radio and barter goods for some fresh scallops to drop down for tuna.

44

19-Fathom Lump

GPS: 38'30.00 / 74'18.50
LORAN: 26855 / 42475
Distance: 38 miles southeast from Cape May Inlet, 41 miles southeast from Townsend's Inlet
Depth: 108 to 150 feet
Target Species: Mako, Thresher and Blue Sharks, Bluefin Tuna, Yellowfin Tuna
Prime Time of Year: May through July (SHK), Late June through September (BFT), July through September (YFT)

For south Jersey anglers, one spot has risen above the rest for inshore pelagic activity, and it comes in the form of the 19-Fathom Lump. The combination of realistic accessibility for mid-range boats mixed with the promising allure of a day trip has vaulted the 19-Fathom Lump into the 20-something craft owner's best friend. The layout of the spot actually reaches 18 fathoms at 108 feet directly on top of the Lump and will drop down between 130 and 150 feet around perimeter. The northwest and northeast sections off of the Lump entertain the greatest depth changes, where the sharp decline hits into the 120 to 150-foot range.

The tale of 19 Fathoms begins with primordial predators—sharks. Captain Bernie Walker of Wavewalker Sportfishing considers 19-Fathom Lump to be his backpocket shark spot. "Without a doubt, the 19 Fathoms is the place I hit for sharking. On a usual trip out, we'll tie into at least one or two makos, we've had 'em to 200 pounds plus here, and a mess of blue sharks all day long. It's usually a ton of action. One June afternoon, we hooked into this one 150 pound high-flying mako. I know makos jump a few times during the fight, but this guy jumped a total of 12 times all around the boat. We found out why he was so juiced up at the dock. This wasn't the first time that he had been hooked! Nor was it the second. In his mouth was a circle hook with jagged heavy mono. My guess, a long-liner rig that he bit through. My hook was deep in his throat, and in his stomach was another very corroded 10/0 hook with about four feet of wire. That mako has been around the block and knew what was going on, so he truly put up a fight for his life."

HOT SHOT TIP
Bluefin tuna hold tight to the bottom in this area. Employ a Tuna Bomb Chum device with a holed paper bag full of butterfish chunks, send it on a line a few feet off the bottom, and then drop your jigs or baits there.

Captain Walker likes to employ an east to west drift over the middle of the Lump when conditions allow, as the greatest variation in ledge depth takes place. The northeast and northwest quadrants surrounding the Lump jump from 21 to 25 fathoms. Makos aren't the only denizens that inhabit the area. Sand eels and spearing schools are familiar for cruising by this

Lump in June through August and their presence attracts tons of tuna. The 19-Fathom Lump lays claim as a sweet summertime bluefin and yellowfin tuna hangout. Bluefin range from football size of 10 to 20 pounds pegging up to 300 pounds, but generally average in the 70 to 100-pound class, as the larger bluefin seem to follow this 20-fathom curve on their migratory path. The smaller bluefin hang in late June and July then get pushed out by their bigger brothers come August. Yellowfin tuna run from 60 to 100 pounds, but show up less frequently than the bluefin. The spot is known primarily as a chunking routine with butterfish and sardines, but another spectacular way to put some tuna onto deck is this: when they mark in the water column, drop a six to 12 ounce Viking or Banana Jig down, one with a slim profile, and jig in four-foot sweeping strokes in front of their noses. More often than not, when you start the tuna on a chunk bite, a well-placed piece of metal will incite a brutal strike.

Oh, and by the way, Captain Bernie's largest shark of his career to date—a 454-pound thresher shark, hit a 10-pound bluefish fillet with the tail left on, drifting right over the 19-Fathom mark. Game on.

45

Hot Dog

GPS: 38'07.00 / 74'17.20
LORAN: 26815 / 42225
Distance: 56 miles southeast from Cape May Inlet
Depth: 110 to 120 feet on top of hill; 180 feet plus less than
  one mile to east
Target Species: Bluefin and Yellowfin Tuna
Prime Time of Year: July through October

You couldn't ask for a more fitting name than the Hot Dog. That's precisely the vibe you get when you hit the spot right. Situated in a west-to-east layout 56 miles southeast of the Cape May Inlet, the Dog is comprised of a bending, elongated lump, strangely reminiscent of a Ballpark frank, that runs from 150 feet on the west side, plateauing up to 115 to 118 feet on the top of the hill in the middle. It then slopes down on the east side to 180 to 220 feet and keeps dropping as you reach out and move eastward toward the Baltimore Canyon. Primarily during the summer months, sand eels follow the 30-fathom contour lines just east of the area and take up residence there. What does that mean for the angler? It means, get the mustard and ketchup, because the Dog gets real tasty.

From 1999 to 2004, the Dog has been a phenomenal bluefin tuna magnet. The recent craze has been sort of a devious siren, calling anglers to the rocks, and has prompted people to risk life and limb taking smaller coastal boats, even 19-foot crafts, loaded with extra fuel and tuna gear to experience the hot bite. Don't follow their lead—make sure your boat is seaworthy for this distance at sea.

HOT SHOT TIP

Keep a case of beer or daily newspapers on board to barter with commercial scallopers in trade for fresh scallop baits.

Many factors contribute to the success stories here for bluefin tuna anglers, with the recent influx of sand eels, but two schools of thought have surfaced that attribute the success of the Hot Dog to two other factors that have affected the seasonal fishery here.

The first theory goes that the flotilla of commercial scallop boats continually work over the area, dragging the bottom and creating a chum slick that ignites the bluefin. It definitely happens and the omnipresent chum slick most surely attracts bluefin to the region. If you're smart, know how to get in contact with a dragger and barter with him for some fresh scallops for hook baits when he's out there. You will be heads and shoulders above the rest of the fleet. The second theory goes like this—with hundreds of anglers targeting bluefin daily at the Dog, the stream of butterfish chum slicks from surrounding boats have "trained" the bluefin not only to come back to the spot year after year, but also to stay there longer than usual. Case in point, during the fall of 2002, the bluefin stayed put well into December.

The key to unlocking the Dog is to set up and establish a chunk slick in the early morning hours. Daybreak bites are most common, and the afternoon bite shows up, but not as often. I hit a trip with Captain John Sowerby of Caveman Sportfishing. Getting there in darkness, the night burned off by the glow of the sun on the horizon, and just before the sun poked over the ocean, we got slammed by three bluefin between 95 and 175 pounds and busted off two more. It all happened before 9 A.M.

Not only is the bluefin bite electric here, but also more yellowfin in the 40 to 70-pound class are showing face on this mid-range spot. Anglers overnighting at the Baltimore Canyon are amending their schedules to come into the Dog for the morning tuna bite.

46

EPH Shoal

GPS: 38'55.60 / 74'56.40
LORAN: 27153 / 42718
Distance: 4.5 miles from Cape May Inlet
Depth: 6 to 30 feet
Target Species: Striped Bass
Prime Time of Year: May, June / September through December

South Jersey anglers know that at Eph Shoal, they can put a blistering on the bass as they move in and out of the Delaware River, passing through the Delaware Bay, back and forth from the Atlantic. Eph Shoal is the virtual tollbooth, the point of entry and exit, where smart anglers set up to intercept them. You know something, before I go into the specs, here's some hard, cold testimony about this Cape May rip.

Late November 2004, I hit up Eph Shoal with Captain Bernie Walker of the *Wavewalker* and we claimed nineteen bass in two hours, with almost just as many missed hits. The bass were from 23 inches to 38 inches long, weighing up to 24 pounds. Textbook day.

Eph Shoal is a 10-minute run out of the Cape May Inlet and roughly a 20-minute ride from the Cape May Canal inlet on the bayside. Eph is the first rip you encounter the famous Cape May Rips coming from the inlet, and is closest to the Cape May coastline, as all the while you are basically fishing under the shadow of the Cape May Lighthouse. The rips of the shoal can be easily distinguished as they are clearly defined by the calm water abruptly running into the rippy, churned water as the depth fluctuates wildly, averaging from running 30 feet or so into 6 to 15 feet of water in an instant. The sands are constantly shifting, so a rip that is there on Eph one day, may be moved around the next day, but generally stays in the same area. Sometimes, grass and seaweed will get sucked in and out with the tides, and it's best to check your line frequently, especially if you feel some unexplained resistance.

The bass in November and December here are gorged with small weakfish, ling, stone crabs, and croakers. They feed tight to the bottom and therefore bucktailing works wonders at Eph. If you have a slow

Backtrolling bucktails at Eph Shoal put the Babcock Boys, (Bob and Mike) into bass.

drift, you can drift with the tide over the bumps. Bouncing two to four-ounce white or chartreuse bucktails tipped with four to eight inch mackerel strips or seven-inch Fin-S fish or Sassy Shads. Mackerel, Rainbow Trout, and Albino White colorations for the plastics will usually elicit a strike. If you have fresh bunker, cut the backs off of them in 4 to 6 inch strips and hook them on the bucktail. Motor over a section of shoal, take the motor out of gear, but keep it running and drift over. Bounce the buck along the bottom. Sounds easy, but the problem at Eph is, the drift at mid-tide can be ridiculously swift, making it almost impossible to hold bottom. If the tide is seriously ripping here, backtrolling is often essential. Using this technique, the captain keeps the boat in gear just in front of a rip and the anglers cast the lure back into the rip and work it out and recast again. I've been in tides that ripped at three knots there and backtrolling was the only way we could get the dang thing on bottom! It's a little bit of extra work, and the captain can't fish as he maintains a position drifting along the edge of the rip ridge, just out of the grip of the three to six-foot swelling rip waves. It's a bit hairy, but worth the effort.

HOT SHOT TIP

When choosing a plastic to put on the bucktail, use one with a paddletail, as the ripping water against it will vibrate the tail and really make the bucktail come alive.

47

Prissywick Shoal

GPS: 38'54.00 / 74'57.00
LORAN: 27120 / 42710
Distance: 5.5 miles out of Cape May Inlet
Depth: 2 to 30 feet
Target Species: Striped Bass
Prime Time of Year: May/June, October through December (STB)

During the late spring and fall, the striped bass electricity in the southern part of the state hits high voltage. Travel down the Garden State Parkway all the way to Exit 0, and you've entered the realm of one of Jersey's prized attractions—Prissywick Shoals.

Prissywick Shoals is part of a region called the Cape May Rips, rich with thick striper activity. The Prissywick shoals are formed when outgoing and incoming tides, mixed with strong tidal situations, course over the sandy bottom create a virtual underwater roller coaster of sandy humps and bumps that shift on every tide. Standing waves form and well up and create whitewater situations of churning, roiling water.

You couldn't ask for better bass fishing structure. The rolling subterranean hills hold bass on each side during the tide phases, as striped bass wait in ambush on the incoming and outgoing tides to suck down bait such as worms, clams, crabs, spearing, small ling and weakfish. Whether it is a high or low tide, incoming or outgoing, the backsides of the humps will hold pods of hungry bass.

Prissywick's reach stretches over roughly a three-mile area just south and a bit east of the Cape May Lighthouse. Out of all the shoals that make up the Cape May Rips, these particular shoals are by far the thinnest of the bunch, constantly shifting their sands with the tides and must be approached with attentive caution. On any given day, the depth of Prissywick can run anywhere from an extremely thin two feet on a dead low tide to around 28 feet on the high tide. And if you are running on a blowout tide from a full moon combined with a westerly wind, you may even see some islands pop up out there, so be careful.

HOT SHOT TIP
Bring a rag to handle and hook eels for a firm grasp. If a bass bumps your eel over a shoal, release the bail and drop it back to him.

The warming spring months of late April through early June trigger the first formidable bass bite, as stripers enter the Delaware River system and prepare to spawn, hiding behind the underwater humps and bumps waiting for baitfish to funnel by. The summertime bite gets quiet, but beginning in early to mid-October, the bass bite goes bananas again as they pass by on their migratory path southward. Eels, herring and spot are the predominant live bait to use here, and one of the greatest qualities is that you can fish the waters daytime or nighttime.

The most popular and productive method to tangle with bass is drifting an eel on a fishfinder rig, consisting of a sinker slide, 80-pound barrel swivel, a four-foot piece of 60-pound fluorocarbon leader, and a size 6/0 Gamakatsu Octopus hook lanced through the jaw and then through one eye of an eel. The sinker weight depends on how much it takes not necessarily to hold bottom, but for the angler to be able to feel the sinker dragging on the bottom and over the humps until it hits bottom again. On average this means a 3 to 4-ounce weight at the beginning or ends of the tide switch. This is the key to fishing Prissywick—always be bouncing the bottom. If you're not, you are simply drag-trolling bait through the upper water column where the bass are not home.

Big bass abound at Prissywick. One June night under a full moon I cast an eel into one of the shoally Rips as we drifted over it and got throttled. Five minutes into the battle, my top-of-the-line, shiny graphite rod snapped, sounding like a 12-gauge gunshot. A half a rod and 20 minutes later, fist over clenched fist, I handlined in a 33 pound striper, reached over the side and slapped him onto the deck. Rod-breaking bass at Prissywick? You bet.

48

60-Foot
Slough

GPS: 39'02.30 / 75'02.50; center, 39'00.50 / 75'02.50
LORAN: 27172 / 42789
Distance: 5 miles from Cape May Canal to tip; 4 miles to center
Depth: 15 to 60 feet
Target Species: Striped Bass, Weakfish, Croakers
Prime Time of Year: May to early June, October and November (STB),
July through October (WEK, CRK)

Big, fat bass. I'm not talking about your usual medium 15 pound linesiders that make up a fun day out. I'm referring to bass that you lose sleep over, the caliber of bass that dreams, or nightmares, depending on your luck, are made of. This drama all plays out at a spot in Delaware Bay named the 60-Foot Slough. The 60-Foot Slough is roughly a 20-minute run north of the Cape May canal, and consists of a mix of mud and sand for bottom. The slough is a deep cut in the bay that averages 30 to 50 feet and bottoms out at 60 feet in the center. The edges rise up to 14 feet, but waver around 15 to 25 feet. This abyss in the middle of nowhere attracts the largest of bass in the bay as they sit to hide and cool down after the summertime warms up the waters. In the fall months of October and November, it really comes alive.

A solid game plan revolves around anchoring up on the west slope or at the tip of the slough and setting out a bunker chunk slick. Four 30 to 50 pound rated rods with 4/0 class reels, spooled with 40-pound test line will do the trick. A fishfinder sleeve, 75 pound barrel swivel, and a six-foot 40-pound fluorocarbon leader with a size 8/0 Gamakatsu Octopus hook is the preferred chunking rig. The wide gap of the Octopus hook will better hold a large bunker chunk and still be able to expose the hook point for a solid set. Start out your slick by cutting up fresh bunker into small, diced pieces with a few small chunks blended in. Send your rods out with thick three to four-inch sections of the bunker and cast them out back to the end, where the slick is settling. Put the clickers on. Every year, stripers reaching 40 pounds come out of this slough. And a few 50 pounders. And a 60 or two. This is the place to score the striper of a lifetime.

Bass are definitely the main attraction here, but other species abound. The 60 Slough is probably one of the most overlooked places to try for black drum, as most anglers hit the Delaware side of the bay in search of the boomers. But the drum do make their way over to the Jersey side in June, and can be effectively targeted with a well-established clam slick. Weakfish and croakers will hold steady all through the summertime. Half to one-ounce white or chartreuse bucktails, tipped with squid strips or sea robin strips and jigged near the bottom, will take a number of hardheads and spiketooths worthy of bragging rights. If you don't get a chance to fish for weakfish or croakers, or think they're not around, just take a look inside one of the bass you bring back home, you'll find your weakfish and croakers there.

HOT SHOT TIP
Throw out either a whole dead bunker or a section of the head and half the body to target the biggest bass.

49

Horseshoe

GPS: 39'03.85 / 75'06.45
LORAN: 27200 / 42820
Distance: 8.5 miles northwest of Cape May Canal
Depth: 13 to 25 feet
Target Species: Black Drum, Striped Bass
Prime Time of Year: Late May through June (BKD, STB)

Boom, Boom, Boom! Listen closely, because you can hear that sound loud and clear from May through June at the Horseshoe. It's the signal that the black drum have moved in and returned to their breeding grounds within Delaware Bay. The Horseshoe is a fitting name, because you can sure as sugar hear these big Clydesdales stamp their feet in the mud and really rustle it up at the Shoe. The Horseshoe lies roughly 8½ miles northwest of the Cape May Canal and is about as far from the Maurice River Inlet inside Delaware Bay. The slough ranges in shallows from 13 to 17 feet on the high edges and sinks to a depth from 21 to 25 feet. It's not a terribly crazy area in terms of ledges and drop-offs, and it isn't a specific slough or hill that stands out from the rest of the bay, but it is a spot black drum and bass find attractive. The eastern edge is a prime spot to hit since the most marked drop-off exists there. Basically, the foundation of the Horseshoe consists of mud with sporadic mussel and clam beds within the area, as well.

Drum go up on the flats to feed during the incoming tide, and mill around the area feeding on the mussels and clams. The recipe for success with the big brutes is to con-

Big, barrel chested black drum can be heard pounding away underwater in Delaware Bay, and some can hit the 90 pound mark such as this behemoth boomer taken on the Wavewalker.

coct a wet and smelly clam chum slick. Anchor up on a flat part, in the range of 13 to 18 feet, and hang a chum pot or two with fresh clams over the side. Start cracking and crushing whole clams and throw them overboard with the shells. Four 50-pound class stand-up rods fixed with 4/0 reels are the muscle you'll need to turn the heads of the big boys. Rig with fishfinder sleeve and a three to five-ounce bank sinker, a four foot section of 50 to 80 pound leader material, and a size 8/0 #92641 Baitholder hook. Find the biggest, sloppiest whole clam that you can pull out of the bag, and hook it a few times through the tongue and then through the body of the clam. Cast out a good 10 to 20 yards behind the boat with two rods, then drop two rods right under the boat. Many times, when the incoming tide is coming up on the slack, the drum will carouse about right under the boat. Turn the radio off, and listen. This is the time when you can actually hear them booming underneath the boat. If you play your cards right, you'll have a hit within a minute or so of hearing them. Drop some fresh clams over the side immediately and watch the rods.

The outgoing and slack tides do work as well, but the incoming is favored here. If you don't tie into any action in over an hour and a half, move. The drum may be following another line or current in the water and you need to get in their general path. It's also worth mentioning that large stripers will also take your clam baits here, so you can have a banner day of bagging a brace of black drum and bass.

HOT SHOT TIP

When the clicker goes off, let the drum run solid for a four count before setting the hook. They are notorious for playing with the clam bait before eating it.

50

Pin Top

GPS: 39'01.08 / 75'07.53
LORAN: 27201 / 42786
Distance: 7 miles from northwest from Cape May canal, 13 miles from Cape May Inlet
Depth: 16 to 36 feet
Target Species: Striped Bass, Black Drum, Weakfish, Fluke
Prime Time of Year: May and June (STB, BKD), June through October (WEK, FLK, CRK)

Within the confines of Delaware Bay, a tiny little spot produces an incredible amount of fish during the year. It's a little hot spot called the Pin Top. Matt Slobodjian of Jim's Bait and Tackle in Cape May says the Pin Top is a mainstay for his patrons who fish the bay. "The Pin Top is basically a tiny little bump on top of a big gully. The spot itself is only about a quarter-mile in circumference and 100 feet in diameter, real small, but it's surrounded by a mess of sloughs and gullies. It sits just southeast of Flounder Alley. On the east side a deep slough cuts across, and on the west side is the Shipping Channel. What you have is a nice little bump in the middle of a bunch of cuts."

Generally, the sloughs around the area run between 30 and 36 feet in depth, and rise up to 20 feet in certain points to their pinnacles. The main spot on the Pin Top, and what gives it its name, is found on the south end, where an underwater hill rises to 16 feet. It sits just southeast of the 16 Buoy, which marks the entrance to Flounder Alley.

The hottest time of the year to hit the Pin Top depends on what type of fish you are targeting. In springtime, it becomes a stopping point for black drum when they inundate the bay. Those anchored up and dropping clams here in and around the sloughs tie up with behemoth black drum and lunker linesiders. Huge black drum to 100 pounds mill around the area, and the stripers that reside here are not your run-of-the-mill schoolies. In fact, many bass topping the 40 to 50-pound range are taken from the area every year.

The area becomes a holding pen for large fluke in the summer. The doormats tend to

It's all about having a line in the water, and then having it get dynamited by some yet unknown monster as Greg Honachefsky hits that feeling we all search for with a smile from ear to ear.

stay in the surrounding cuts, and Slobodjian recommends, "Drift over the edges of the slough, come on up over the Top, and drift over the other side on an east to west drift. You'll find the flatties hanging on the edges. All throughout the summer you can also find hardheaded croakers and 2 to 5-pound weak-fish moving through the underwater channels."

HOT SHOT TIP
Work in and around the deep gullies, bouncing around the Pin Top with 1 to 2 ounce white bucktails for large fluke, weakfish and croakers.

Come fall, striped bass take up residence once again, and those who target larger fish will chunk fresh bunker on fishfinder rigs to pull out a respectable stringer of bass. The main technique for the Pin Top is to anchor on up near the Pin itself and create either a clam or bunker chunk chum slick to bring the bass and drum to the boat. The ensuing slick wafting down the slopes and into the sloughs will bring up many a hungry fish.

"People seem to love to fish the Pin Top, yet it remains uncrowded," says Slobodjian. "Mostly in spring and fall, my customers always bring in some nice bass and drum from the area. It's definitely a lock in if you play your cards right."

LAST CAST

As much fun as this book was to write, it was also a ton of hard work; researching data, organizing interviews, finding the time to actually write it, and so on. But it isn't nearly as much hard work as local New Jersey fishing organizations the Recreational Fishing Alliance (RFA), and the Jersey Coast Anglers Association (JCAA), put in to defend our fisheries, and to insure a viable and fair representation for recreational fishermen. You can join both of these organizations by checking out www.joinrfa.org or www.jcaa.org. From the countless hours of fun and adventure you'll inevitably have out there plying the waters of the Atlantic, I also recommend making a fishing log of your own to chart, track and document every bit of information that you may run across, not only to use as a technical guide, but to relive your experience for years to come. Believe me, it's worth it. But above all, take the time to wonder and experience the Atlantic, the back bay, or the pond at the end of the road. Introduce a child or a friend or a significant other to the water, and make sure he or she has a fishing rod in hand. If we don't encourage and promote our fine sport, it may get lost in the mix of the rat race of this world, and then the true beauty of a bluefish's pull, a striper's surface strike, a yellowfin's electric colors, will be but a shadow. Besides, what's better than a tug on the end of the line. Exactly.

To contribute or sponsor a wreck on New Jersey's Artificial Reef Program, contact the NJ Division of Fish and Wildlife at Nacote Creek Station, P.O. Box 418, Port Republic, NJ 08241 or dial up Bill Figley at 609-748-2020.

BIBLIOGRAPHY

Shipwrecks of the Atlantic, Bill Davis, (The Fisherman Library 1991)

A Guide to Fishing and Diving New Jersey Reefs, (NJ Division of Fish and Wildlife & The Fisherman)

Atlantic Wrecks, John Raguso, (The Fisherman Library, 1992)

www.NJscuba.com, (Captain Steve Nagiewicz 2003)

INDEX